Sweet Relief

from the everyday
NARCISSIST

Melissa Schenker & Tina Moody

LIVE OAK
BOOK COMPANY

Published by Live Oak Book Company
Austin, TX
www.liveoakbookcompany.com

Copyright ©2012 Melissa Schenker and Tina Moody

Distributed by Live Oak Book Company

For ordering information or special discounts for bulk purchases, please contact Live Oak Book Company at PO Box 91869, Austin, TX 78709, 512.891.6100.

Design and composition by Bucko Design and Greenleaf Book Group LLC
Cover design by Bucko Design

Publisher's Cataloging-In-Publication Data
(Prepared by The Donohue Group, Inc.)

Schenker, Melissa.
    Sweet relief from the everyday narcissist / Melissa Schenker and Tina Moody. -- 1st ed.

    p. ; cm.

    Issued also as an ebook.
    ISBN: 978-1-936909-41-4

    1. Narcissism--Popular works. 2. Interpersonal relations. I. Moody, Tina. II. Title.

BF575.N35 S34 2012
616.85854   2012934516

Print ISBN: 978-1-936909-41-4

eBook ISBN: 978-1-936909-43-8

First Edition

Contents

"Being involved with a narcissist is draining. So many things about it don't make sense to most of us, and without a solid understanding of how narcissists work, we are vulnerable to falling into the same traps again."

Introduction

This book is intended for people struggling with a difficult or confusing relationship. It is for people who are in a relationship in which the other person claims so much attention that you may lose sight of yourself. This book is intended for people who are looking for insight and help in understanding and managing the challenges of this relationship.

Each of us brings our own personality and dynamics to our relationships—but some people bring with them destructive and confusing behaviors. For those of us who've lived with this confusion, it's helpful to know that there are some personality types—types that can be identified—that create certain predictable and destructive patterns in their relationships. This book deals specifically with the problems caused by people who are narcissistic and self-absorbed to the point they are impaired in their ability to connect with and care for others.

■ *This book will address a number of important topics:*

- What is narcissism?
- How does narcissism develop?
- What can I expect if I'm in relationship with a narcissist?
- Why is it so difficult and confusing to be in a relationship with a narcissist?
- How can I take care of myself if my partner in our relationship is a narcissist?

One of the co-authors of this handbook is a licensed professional therapist and the other is a work/life coach; both of us have had personal and professional experience with narcissistic relationships.

We wrote this book believing our knowledge and experiences can help others understand their own relationships with the overly self-absorbed. We hope to help others learn and to help them consider how to take care of themselves in light of what they learn. Being involved with a narcissist is draining. So many things about it don't make sense to most of us, and without a solid understanding of how narcissists work, we are vulnerable to falling into the same traps again and miss the opportunity to build satisfying relationships.

Without understanding and insight, we may persist in methods of relating that don't work and that leave us dissatisfied, upset, or even in danger. Coming out of a tough relationship, we're likely to blame ourselves, or to blame the other person. Our hope is that with this book you may come to an understanding of narcissism's destructive relationship dynamics and come to forgive yourself for your confusion and mistakes, move forward to take care of yourself, and perhaps even find compassion for the narcissist in your life.

This book is not intended to be a quick fix. It is not a license to label a troublesome person as a "narcissist" in order to dismiss them, to "call them out," or to expect them—or you yourself—to make swift, reactive changes. Our hope is that you will use this book to take an introspective look at your relationships, yourself, and your situation so that you can make wise, thoughtful decisions about who you are and who you want to be with.

The pace of this book is deliberate, steady and intentional, with the aim of helping you develop a deeper awareness of the dynamics in your relationships so that you can begin to make thoughtful changes. This will help you move forward toward manageable and lasting ways of being in relationships. Our suggestions are very practical, yet the results can be profound.

Professional assistance is often useful if you conclude that you are (or have been) in a significant relationship with a narcissist. Consulting a coach or therapist may be helpful. Search for a professional well-versed in the ways of the self-absorbed; they can assist you as you negotiate the confusing world of the narcissist.

An important note: As you begin to develop an understanding of the particular relationship that is troubling you, be thoughtful and sensible about what you're learning. Declaring to a person, "You are a narcissist," will most likely result in your being casually dismissed, or worse, evoking scorn or anger. Taking good care of yourself is the goal: It is wise to take your time, learn all you can, and then decide upon a reasonable course of action. This book is not meant to diagnose or blame anyone. It is intended to inform you and give you tools to care for yourself and others in your life wisely.

We will alternate genders from chapter to chapter. Narcissism is not limited only to one gender, so to keep the text linguistically simple we will designate a female as the narcissist in one chapter and a male as a narcissist in the next.

There are many personal stories peppered throughout the book. We are extremely grateful to all those who shared their experiences with us. (Of course, all names have been changed to care for their privacy.)

The book is organized to lead you through stages of understanding in a progressive way, focusing in a rotating fashion on the narcissist and then on you and your experience.

Chapter 1 is designed to help you know if this book is for you. A simple quiz will help you assess your relationship. Lists of some basic elements of the narcissist will clue you in as to whether narcissism may be the problem in your relationship. If you find that this quiz and the lists do not ring true for your relationship, then keep looking to find the source of the difficulties. Not everyone is a narcissist, so this book may not be relevant to you.

Chapter 2 explains what narcissism is and how it develops. Since the word narcissism is popular and widely used, there can be confusion about exactly what narcissism is and what it means.

Chapter 3 shifts from focusing on narcissism and the narcissist and instead explores your own experience of your relationship. Being on the receiving side of such a relationship carries with it some specific characteristics. Considering what the experience is like for you might help you discern whether narcissism is at the heart of your relationship or not. Simply knowing that other people experience something similar can be a relief.

Chapter 4 turns back to a more in-depth look at the basic dynamics of a narcissist's relationships. The framework of narcissism affects relationships in some very particular ways, and this chapter examines these many elements.

Chapter 5 returns the focus to you, the person in relationship with a narcissist. This chapter takes a look at why being in a relationship with a narcissist is so crazy-making. This chapter goes below the surface to explain the patterns that makes the relationship go from enjoyable to crazy-making.

Chapter 6 focuses on how you can take care of yourself and suggests practical strategies for dealing with a narcissist.

Chapter 7 looks toward your future. It will help you explore what you want next; to figure out whether you want to maintain your relationship or end it. This chapter will help you understand how you can begin to heal.

We hope this book will provide understanding, companionship, and relief for you, the reader. Understanding the patterns that underlie your relationship with a narcissist is essential to making change. Knowing that you are not alone in your confusion and pain—that there are others out there who share your experience is, in itself, relieving. While it may not at first be obvious how to proceed with what you have learned about narcissistic relationships, knowing these things can be important in accompanying you toward whatever lies ahead for you. We hope this book will give you information and insights to help you on your way. The work may be challenging, but the rewards can be great.

"Initially most narcissists are quite likable, charming even, and it's easy to get into the relationship without noticing the warning signs, even if you've become educated about narcissism."

Chapter 1 | *Signs of Narcissism*

This chapter is designed to give you the simple, basic information you need to determine if narcissism is a factor in your relationship. The basics are the same whether the relationship is romantic, family, friend, colleague, co-worker, or anyone else. Relationally debilitating self-absorption is not confined to one gender.

A Brief Look at the Other Person

At first glance, narcissism is difficult to detect. It is easy to get involved with a narcissist without knowing. Initially most narcissists are quite likable, charming even, and it's easy to get into the relationship without noticing the warning signs, even if you've become educated about narcissism. Most clues in the beginning of a relationship are obscure. Once you develop awareness, however, the signs can be more evident. A little further into the relationship, the signs can be increasingly clear.

■ *A list of things to look for in a narcissist:*

- Seems likable, is generally charming or highly engaging with people who pique his interest, especially in the early days of the relationship.

- Prefers to be the center of attention, the life of the party, the expert, the star.

- Does not ask many questions about what is going on with other people. If he does ask questions, he doesn't listen well to answers. Your activities, your opinions, your past, your emotional state will not get much attention. A narcissist who asks after your welfare is generally after only short answers. One follow-up question is usually as far as it will go. One question about you per conversation is normal for a narcissist.

- Forgets things you've told him about yourself, details of your past, your likes or dislikes, your plans.

- Brags about himself or his accomplishments.

- Name-drops.

- Lights up when praised.

- Doesn't consider someone else's point of view; can't put himself in someone else's "shoes."

- Has few real friends, although there may be a lot of people around him. Most friends are work related. He doesn't take the initiative to maintain relationships beyond the initial stages.

- Is unaware of and unconcerned about his impact on another person. For example, he's unaware and unapologetic about his impact on your schedule.

- Expects you to accommodate him but does not reciprocate.

- Insists on his way and can be difficult to deal with if he doesn't get it.

- Can be a workaholic, or a "one-trick pony" of sorts, and has few, if any, interests outside of that singular talent.

- Is image-conscious; likes status symbols and seeks to adopt the accepted trappings of his particular social or work scene.

- Dismisses viewpoints that contradict his opinions. May ask for your preference but will still do it his way.

- Does things primarily because they look good or are impressive, rather than because he enjoys them or cares about them.

- Compares himself to other successful people; either comes up short and uses it as motivation to strive, or comes up as better and is self-satisfied.

- Makes agreements, but does not necessarily keep them. Frequently neglects to inform others that he's no longer going to keep an agreement.

- Meets your anger with his own ire which diverts attention from addressing your issues.

- Likes to associate with those he admires.

- Is readily sensitive to perceived slights.

- Is very sensitive to criticism.

- Does things "for" other people—but without finding out what the other person might actually like. If a narcissist is told by the other person what she really wants, he frequently will hear it as criticism and may go on to do something entirely different.

- Is unable to access any insight about his own emotional state without being led. He may identify his emotions but usually only after someone else has made observations about him. He will discuss these emotions or conditions, but only after someone else has identified them. For instance, a narcissist may say he's "depressed" but only after someone else has named it.

- Is not able to articulate his own emotional needs, nor is he able to take action on his own behalf to meet his own emotional needs.

A Look at You

Another way to consider whether or not you are in relationship with a narcissist is to look at what is going on with you and your own reactions to the other person.

There is a basic framework most narcissists use to operate in the world. As a result, there are common elements in how most of us react when we are involved with them. Also, there are some common characteristics among people who are likely to become involved in a personal relationship with a narcissist. Whether you are in a troublesome work relationship or a difficult personal relationship, the dynamics and your reactions are likely to be the same. Here are some things to look for in yourself.

■ *A list of things to look for in you. Are you:*

- Easygoing, flexible, not overly attached to having things your way?

- Averse to conflict or, conversely, thrive on conflict?

- Think the person in question often acts selfishly?

- Dissatisfied with the relationship?

- Often unable to address issues of concern to you because of his resistance to talking about them?

- Committed to making the relationship last long term (in the case of a love relationship), or for the duration of a project (at work)?

- Confused by what has happened to the relationship after it started out so well?

- Delighted when this person actually does turn positive attention your way?

- Comfortable sharing attention or happy with having attention deflected away from you?

- Happy to enjoy attention that comes your way from being with this person?

- Keeping concerns about this relationship to yourself?

- Confused about what happens in the relationship on a daily basis, and disconcerted about what has happened to the relationship overall?

- The only initiator of emotional or strategic tasks required to keep the relationship moving smoothly?

- Adept at dealing with "difficult" or unavailable personalities?

- Someone who grew up with an emotionally distant, domineering, or self-centered parent or in a chaotic environment?

- Highly self-sufficient, good at taking care of business, or conversely highly dependent?

- Able to get many of your needs met outside of this relationship?

- Taking more than your share of responsibility for problems in the relationship, thinking there is something you should be able to do better that would make the relationship work?

- Frustrated in your attempts to convey your desires, to be seen or heard? Do you try to convince, cajole, or insist that you ought to be considered?

- Skilled at strategizing the best plan for sharing information, believing that if you could just say it right, you might be understood, or get satisfaction?

- Likely to refrain from sharing personal good news in order to avoid having it deflated?

- Quiet and reserved in the presence of the narcissist while in social situations?

Quiz

Take this quiz about the behavior of the narcissist in your relationship. It addresses the way he is likely to behave in an established relationship, rather than in one that is new and just developing. Your answers will help you identify whether you are involved with a narcissist. Give one of the following values to each item below: 1 = never, 2 = seldom, 3 = occasionally, 4 = usually, 5 = always.

■ *Does this person:*

_____ Charm newcomers?
_____ Engages in new relationships quickly and easily?
_____ Light up when praised?
_____ Seem most vibrant when in performance mode?
_____ Have a tendency to bring conversations back around to his latest activities, interests, opinions, or achievements?
_____ Want what he wants regardless of the consequences?
_____ Get angry when you express your own anger or

dissatisfaction, thereby diverting attention away from
your feelings and toward his own?

_____ Forget or dismiss things you've shared that are
important to you or about you?

_____ Do what suits him regardless of agreements you've
made, or social/workplace norms?

_____ Fail to apologize for upsetting behaviors, or when he
does apologize, seem insincere?

_____ Neglect to maintain a network of friends outside of
work or one important hobby?

_____ Have trouble imagining what it's like to be in someone
else's shoes?

_____ Withdraw communication or physically isolate when
criticized, or when he feels criticized?

_____ Seek frequent assurances of your physical whereabouts
when discontent?

❚ *Now, some questions for you. Do you:*

_____ Find that this person makes plans without including
you in the process?

_____ Realize that you are the one to start the conversation if
there are issues between you that need to be addressed?

_____ Find that you avoid conflicts with this person because
when you stand up for yourself it leads to aggravation?

_____ Realize that your viewpoint gets ignored or dismissed?

_____ Notice that you are skeptical about relying on
agreements that he makes?

_____ Find that it is easier to relinquish the spotlight to this
person rather than try to share it?

_____ Notice that you are really good at taking care of things,
picking up the slack?

—— Put up with relationship problems because you have hope?

—— Find yourself somewhat confused about what you want for yourself?

—— Notice you are skilled at getting along with people generally considered difficult by others?

—— Feel ineffective in this relationship?

—— Feel that your conversations about logistics are often thwarted?

—— Get frustrated that this person doesn't take care of things you expect him to do?

Scoring

Under 80: Unlikely that narcissism is the issue you are facing. Read on purely if you're interested.

81-107: Likely that you are dealing with a relationship where narcissism is at play. Read on to discern more.

108-135: Most likely, narcissism plays a starring role in your relationship issues. Read on to understand what's going on and how to take care of yourself.

If this information strikes a chord, then this book is for you. Please be aware there may be other reasons for a troubled relationship. You may be in a relationship that is difficult for you, but where no personality disorder exists. Or you may be dealing with some other personality disorder.

Studies show that people with narcissistic personality disorder may also have borderline personality disorder or anti-social personality disorder (aka sociopathy/psychopathy). If you are dealing with a troubling relationship, it may serve you well to also research those. Addictions and depression can be companions to any of these. Also, narcissism exists along a spectrum, so people may exhibit relationship-debilitating traits of narcissism, but maybe would not be diagnosed with a full personality disorder.

The need to understand the relationship problems discussed here can arise at any time in your life, or at any point in a relationship. You might be in a new relationship that has some inexplicable dynamics or niggling hesitations. It could be that something in the external circumstances of the relationship has changed, something in you may have changed, or that the relationship has simply evolved to the point that things you once considered trivial are now quite troublesome. Whatever has brought you to this point, understanding narcissism can be very helpful.

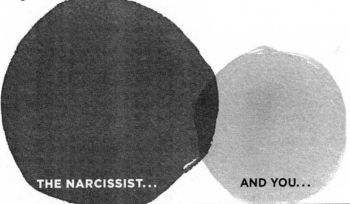

THE NARCISSIST...	AND YOU...
Enjoys being the center of attention	Relinquish spotlight rather than share it
Displays a short attention span to the needs of others	Are capable of picking up other people's slack
Withdraws or isolates when criticism is felt	Avoid conflict
Dissmisses or forgets things important to you	Feel hope that things will change
	Feel confused about your own personal needs
Fails to apologize for upsetting behaviors	Able to get along with "difficult" people
Unable to see the other person's perspective	

"Awareness of the basics of how narcissism develops can help you have compassion for the narcissist and provide insight that allows you to better manage a relationship."

Chapter 2 | *Narcissism Explored*

Before you can understand how a narcissist functions in a relationship, you need a basic working knowledge of just what narcissism is. Many of us have a vague notion of narcissism because it's so widely discussed in our popular culture. But more depth on the subject is necessary if you are struggling with an important relationship, whether at home or work.

The information in this section draws primarily on the work of Erik Erikson on the stages of psychosocial development, Mary Ainsworth's writing on attachment theory, and Dan Siegel's work on parenting.

Healthy Development

In order to appreciate how a person develops narcissism, an understanding of how an emotionally healthy person develops is useful for comparison. Below is a cursory description of the first two stages of child development. For more in-depth information, there are many good books available on child development at your local bookstore or online. For our purposes, knowing the basics of healthy development can illuminate what goes awry in the narcissist's early development.

Many early factors, perceptions, experiences, and memories influence relationships in adulthood. This section focuses specifically on those generally thought to have the most impact on creating the relational framework of the overly self-absorbed.

Early Childhood: Groundwork for Trust and Autonomy

The first three years of life provide the foundation for critical elements of personality development. During this period, a child progresses through two significant developmental stages that create the foundation for the adult this child will become.

A child who emerges emotionally healthy has had the opportunity to develop trust, security, basic optimism, and a sense of autonomy, or awareness of herself as separate from her primary caregiver. She is able to perceive the difference between herself and others. She knows "I am not you." A child who emerges less healthy has the ground prepared for narcissistic personality disorder or other personality problems to emerge later in life. She emerges fearful and insecure. She suffers from shame and self-doubt and remains emotionally merged with her primary caregiver. Her template is, "You and I are one and the same."

In the first stage of development, babies express their needs and desires loud and clear through their behavior and their voice. They experience their needs in every cell of their body, in a very visceral way. If the caregiver empathizes with the infant's experience of need and responds accordingly, the need is met and she is satisfied. The non-verbal conversation between expressed need and the satisfaction of that need produces a deep bond between the child and caregiver. This repeated experience provides the fundamentals for healthy relationship patterns later in life.

The infant relies on caregivers to provide consistent responses to her basic needs and wants. She's busy practicing the primary functions of her new environment in the physical world. Breathing, digestion, elimination, rapid growth, and brain development dominate this time. Later, as she grows, she takes the next step, exploring the world beyond the cradle of loving arms. Having caregivers attend to her with empathy and appropriate responses demonstrates this new outside world to be a safe, reliable place in which to thrive. Trust develops.

In the second stage a toddler is actively engaged in exploring her world, all the while maintaining close contact with her primary caregiver for guidance and affirmation of her existence. When it comes to exploring her environment, a toddler counts on her caregivers to be touchstones of comfort and security. She returns for reassurance, moves out to play, returns again for reassurance, going a little further away each time and staying away a little longer.

As the positive reinforcement of these processes repeat, the child maintains her sense of trust and adds confidence. The child becomes more and more sure of her abilities. It is through successfully repeating this process over and over that a child gradually separates from a caregiver and "individuation" is advanced. With trust in her pocket, exercising her capacities is an exciting adventure. Eventually, this ongoing practice of coming into her own leads to accepting herself as an individual distinct from her caregiver.

Toddlers experience life fully and completely, stopping to pay attention to the smallest things and feeling joy and sadness, anger and fear with a full-body intensity. From her limited perspective, she is omnipotent and powerful, and others exist solely to take care of her. This is because early in life she doesn't see herself as separate from the caregivers who hold the reins of her existence in their hands. She is aware of her existence through her continued nonverbal emotional back and forth with her caregiver. Their compassionate interactions allow her to develop a sense that she exists as a separate being, and that she is safe and okay as a separate being in her world.

At this stage, a child's perceptions, sensations and emotions are her only operating framework. She lives them through her body. She feels praise all the way to her core, and it leaves her beaming with pleasure and certainty. But, during this stage of development, she also frequently hears "NO" as her caregiver seeks to keep her safe and guide her. This sort of correction, criticism, or scolding is also felt as a full body experience. A toddler who does something wrong and is corrected with proportion appropriate to the mistake is able to handle the redirection with only slight distress, or with upset that does not endure long. A toddler who is stopped from doing something risky and is shown the risk can learn to correct her own behavior. A toddler who is roundly scolded, blamed, or shamed, risks developing in troubling ways.

Helping a young toddler return to a sense of security after receiving an intense, humiliating correction for an action that is undesirable or socially inappropriate is as much the caregiver's task as the correction itself. To recover from intense feeling a toddler needs help from her caregiver. Compassionate guidance and acceptance of the child's limitations are important to aid recovery from the redirection. A caregiver who maintains connection through a child's misdeeds serves the bigger needs of the child. Reassurance that she, as a being in the world, is valuable in spite of her misdeeds is what is necessary. An upset, humiliated child needs a caregiver's loving embrace to guide her back to a sense of feeling okay and accepted. When the caregiver helps the child stay connected during the correction process, a healthy child learns it is okay to make mistakes; she will be okay moving out into the world and interacting with other people.

A sense of safety and confidence is key to a child's ability to move away from the caregiver to a more independent stance in the world. A healthy sense of self develops when she has a caregiver sensitive to and perceptive of her needs, and calmly accepting of her mistakes. With this continuity in her relating, she is safe to experiment with separation and distance and can rely on her caregiver as a home base for emotional refueling and direction. In navigating her bigger world she moves toward becoming a distinct self linked to, but not merged with, her caregiver or others. As long as the caregiver is emotionally tuned in and compassionately responsive most of the time, the child will feel safe to move away further and further, both physically and emotionally.

Throughout the ensuing years, she will rely on this framework to repeat her experiments of tolerable distance until she is capable of developing as a separate, independent individual. She will sometimes long for oneness, but she will also have a strong innate motivation to be independent with all her own unique gifts and graces. Learning to regulate her bad feelings through the guidance of her caregivers, she will become aware that she sometimes does "good" and sometimes does "bad," but that she is lovable in the face of it all.

As an adult, she will retain a sense of her own wholeness. She will be able to entrust herself to the relational arms of others for communion. She will not cling to her loved ones in desperation, but rather will revel in the delight of temporary unity and then return to her own self-reliance until the next reunion.

The Spectrum: Healthy to Unhealthy Narcissism

There are a lot of reasons narcissism is confusing. It's not just the dynamics that can confuse a person, but the concepts and theories can also. Narcissism gets talked about a lot, but most of us do not have an adequate understanding of what it is or is not. For instance, we hear that there is such a thing as "healthy narcissism." Or we hear things like "everyone is a narcissist to a certain extent." We hear that narcissism is self-focus—but everyone has self-focus, it's necessary for self-care. We offer this information to bring some clarity.

Each and every one of us goes through developmental stages to distinguish our self from the selves of others. And while we are all ultimately connected, it is our distinctiveness that adds to the richness and subtle shadings that make life vibrant. It takes an intense self-focus to successfully negotiate the processes of knowing who we are and come out increasingly differentiated on the other side. So during the course of our development, particularly around age two and the teen years, we are all narcissistic to some degree. The adult with "healthy narcissism" is the person who is able to understand herself as a separate being, linked to, but different from others. She is increasingly able to identify and supply her own needs while acknowledging that others may have needs too, although they may be different from hers. This person connects with others by exposing her authentic, individuated self for rapport and resourcing of her own needs. She can move into intimacy and shift back to independence and navigate various points in between.

The person with narcissistic personality disorder has not been able to successfully negotiate these stages of distinction. She is held as a captive being psychologically merged with others at all times. This is unhealthy narcissism.

Yet, between healthy and unhealthy narcissism there are many way stations. Healthy narcissism allows for a self-focus and an awareness of others that may come and go; it creates relationships where the other person is acknowledged and reciprocity is possible. Emotional sophistication and health varies and some people may be narcissistic or self-absorbed only from time to time. Some periods of life call for this, and it is appropriate and unavoidable. Thinking of narcissism as a spectrum with emotional health on one end and fully developed narcissism on the other is helpful. On the healthy side of the spectrum people are able to have relationships with a give and take. On the other side are people who, as narcissists, lack the ability to empathize with others.

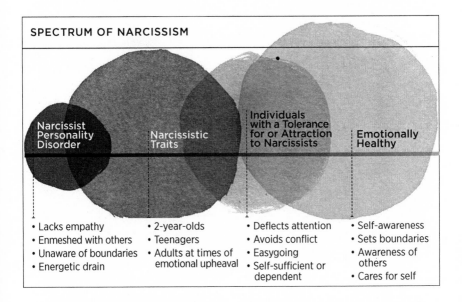

SPECTRUM OF NARCISSISM

Narcissist Personality Disorder	Narcissistic Traits	Individuals with a Tolerance for or Attraction to Narcissists	Emotionally Healthy
• Lacks empathy • Enmeshed with others • Unaware of boundaries • Energetic drain	• 2-year-olds • Teenagers • Adults at times of emotional upheaval	• Deflects attention • Avoids conflict • Easygoing • Self-sufficient or dependent	• Self-awareness • Sets boundaries • Awareness of others • Cares for self

Narcissistic Development

The framework that allows narcissism to emerge later in life is created between the ages of birth and three years of age. A child unable to navigate through this period successfully fails to develop a sense of autonomy for herself as a separate individual. She maintains her earliest template for relating and risks growing into a self-absorbed adult.

During infancy and very early toddlerhood, a child has no awareness that her primary caregiver is a being separate from her. Her needs are felt and expressed non-verbally—she's too young to be capable of words and too undeveloped to name her wants and desires. It is as if she is the only being in the world, and as if her needs are paramount above all else. If the primary caregiver is emotionally unavailable for whatever reason (lack of emotional awareness, grief, addiction, personality disorder, depression, or myriad other possibilities), then the infant's primitive need for connection and reassurance that it's okay to explore the world independently is thwarted. When this happens, the baby fails to advance her development of a separate self; she fails to separate. She is forever merged, enmeshed, with others. She continues to rely on others to respond to her non-verbally expressed needs and emotions. She has the neural pathways set for narcissism to emerge in later life.

Lack of reliable emotional connection between a baby and caregiver impacts the developing child. The template for an adult narcissist is laid by a child's natural reactions to her circumstances.

▌ *The basic patterns are:*

- a lack of awareness of others existing as separate from herself, a vigilant awareness of others (especially in the initial stages of relating)—being highly attuned/people pleasing,

- attention-seeking (either admiration or criticism),

- passive and reactive in her emotional life,

- tone deaf to the emotional life and needs of others,

- hypersensitive to criticism or being perceived as rejected,

- use of isolation to repair and regroup, and

- managing by relying on specific rules for behavior.

Without enough experience exploring the world with the touchstone of a caregiver to provide assurance and guidance about her safety, her *is-ness* continues to reside in the caregiver, and for the narcissist-to-be, it never shifts to reside in herself. Since she feels uncertain and unsafe and knows that other more capable beings are sometimes present and can provide her with what she needs to survive and be safe, she learns all sorts of tactics to monitor and capture the attention of that key person. This means that at a pre-conscious, non-verbal level this child is highly aware of the moods and behaviors of this other person. Hypervigilance, people-pleasing, and attention-seeking behaviors are the result, especially when she feels threatened. She intuitively grasps that in order to get the attention and reassurance of her caregiver, it is best to be pleasing; show up bigger, or stronger, or smarter. Basically, she has to work hard for recognition in whatever way is pleasing to her caregiver. A driving force materializes. It comes from this attempt to reconnect; striving for that mirrored experience with her caregiver. By maintaining a vigilant awareness of her caregiver, her ability to focus on herself and her world is impaired. She remains merged with her caregiver because she is not free to roam. She learns, too, that to please others is the basis for her existence. She learns the rules of the road for getting attention. She creates a playbook for behavior and getting attention that she relies on, and continues to develop, throughout her life.

She also learns that negative attention can be as viable a tool as positive attention, and it's frequently an easier way to get that life-affirming connection with a caregiver. So a grown up narcissist has learned in toddlerhood to try to capture attention of the admiring sort "look at me for what I'm capable of doing now" and of the negative sort "I know you will pay attention to me when I run out into the street." She learns that negative attention is better than no attention at all. If she cannot get attention for accomplishments, she'll get attention for trouble. Negative attention will also validate her existence. A driving need to be admired or corrected stays with this person for life.

Unwittingly, the child may invite problems by provoking negative attention. If the caregiver is able to provide correction without regularly shaming the child, then the child learns appropriate behaviors and develops along a healthy continuum. Successful correction uses a calm tone and provides concrete information about what to do. For instance, "Amy, please put that ketchup bottle back on the table. It might break and spill ketchup all over you and the table if you keep fiddling with it." If the caregiver uses shame or isolation as a tool to get compliance, then difficulty is designed into the child's neural networks. Correction without shame allows a child to know she did something wrong. Correction with shame invites a child (or anyone for that matter) to feel wrong at a being level. Rather than "I did something unacceptable," the child interprets the correction as "I am unacceptable." If shame is repeatedly used by an adult as a tool to create compliance in a child, patterns are laid in the developing mind, which add to the narcissistic template being created for that child.

Caretaker behavior that invites a child into feeling shamed can be of a few different sorts. If it happens infrequently, with the adult remembering to follow it quickly with apology and comfort, the child can develop in a healthy manner. If the myriad ways of shaming are used repeatedly, the template of "I'm wrong" and self-isolation get created and the seeds of narcissism are planted and may bloom later in life.

■ *The problematic caregiver behaviors include:*

- **Disdain through tone, intent, or content.** Disdain is a shaming stance, indicating there's something wrong with the whole person not just with her mistake. Tone of voice can transform innocuous words into a reproach of the person. For instance, "Amy, put that down" can be clean direction or a shaming dependent upon how it's delivered. Simple phrases can belittle, for instance, "Amy, you know better than to play with a ketchup bottle."

- **Universalizing a mistake or unwelcome behavior.** "Bad girl" is about the whole being, not the action taken. There's no room for correction in a universal message, just an invitation for the child to assume he's all bad and there's nothing he can do about it. Conversely, "good girl" is just as confusing because it, too, is universal. This caregiver makes the child all good or all bad, and gives the child little guidance on how to be good but make a correctable mistake.

- **Banishment from the caretaker's presence or overparenting.** "Amy, look, now you've gone and dropped the ketchup! What a mess I have to clean up! Go to the corner for a time out." This communicates, "You are bad and furthermore I don't want you around me because of your badness and the trouble you cause." Another troubling behavior is the adult who shows off a child to get the reflected glow of approval, or who pays such minute attention to the child that an internal guidance ability doesn't develop.

- **An emotionally explosive response that overwhelms the child.** This sort of reaction from an all-powerful adult communicates, "I am upset and on the edge and it's your fault." It feels (and is) dangerous at a core level to a dependent child. A child will naturally shrink and isolate from over-powering actions by the caregiver. The unsophisticated mind will assume it's her fault, there is something wrong with her, for provoking such an upset.

- **Scolding that communicates, "You embarrass me."** In this case, the adult is enmeshed with the child and feels the child's behavior as if it is their own; as if the child's mistakes are the mistakes of the adult. This is the adult who needs the child to behave in certain ways in order to take care of the emotional well being of the adult. Sometimes the corrections such an adult uses seem mild, but the underlying message of "You must be different in order to take care of me and so I can be comfortable" remains (and is intricately confusing to the developing mind). For instance, "Amy, look at you now. You're a mess with that ketchup all over you" meaning . . . 'I'm embarrassed and I look bad.'

- **Failure to provide guidance and feedback in the real world of social interactions and emotional management.** During a time of upset, correction, high fear, or high excitement, the caregiver needs to be there with the child and tolerate the discomfort along with her, and gently guide her back to equilibrium.

All of these caregiver behaviors invite the child into feeling wrong at a being level, rather than wrong for behavior that can be changed. They disconnect the child from the adult and force the child to comfort herself in isolation and through her imagination. This pattern becomes the template underlying her behavior throughout life.

For a child in this situation, negative attention and negative consequences come as a double-edged sword. On one side is the intense emotional contact so longed for and on the other edge she experiences shame. She gets attention but doesn't understand that she's made a mistake. She concludes that she IS the mistake. As a result, shame permeates her being. The experience is overwhelming. It's an agonizing place. She needs a compassionate caregiver to invite her out of her isolation, demonstrating love and acceptance even though she behaved unacceptably. Basically, she needs an ally to recover from shame. Frequent doses of shame, combined with a lack of compassionate assistance in recovering from the experience, affects emotional development negatively. An immature mind experiencing repeated bouts of shame without repair, copes by splitting the "bad" part of the personality from the "good" part and forever seeks to keep these spheres segregated. Her implicit memory builds on that notion that "I am either perfect or no good at all."

The use of isolation to emotionally repair and regroup comes about because a baby with a consistently disconnected primary caregiver is left to her own devices much of the time, or because the caregiver uses overwhelming shame as a learning/punishment tool. The child develops a pattern of isolating herself because there is no satisfaction in attempting to relate. She feels in danger at an elemental level, because she's relatively alone and vulnerable in an unknown world. Insecurity is a constant undertone, and isolation is the only tactic she has for comfort. In her isolation, her imagination takes over and props her back up so she can face the world again.

Eventually, she will peek out of her isolated emotional cocoon and seek to be connected again. Implicitly knowing that admiration is more pleasant than criticism, yet either response is better than nothing at all, she aims for the connection that sustains her, hopefully in a more pleasing light. Attention from her caregiver evolves as the guiding star in her life. She seeks the caregiver's continual confirmation of her existence and approval of her behavior. If she can't get emotional connection, she will substitute physical proximity. She becomes intuitively vigilant, scanning her caregiver to ascertain what is needed to get the caregiver's attention or approval. She will adapt herself to what seems worthy in the eyes of her caregiver. Unwelcome rejection leads to unbearable isolation from her caregiver, but the caregiver remains her center of reference, inextricable from who she is. Failing to have her trust needs met, she still craves the comfort of being one with her caregiver, being recognized and thus granted assurance that she does exist; that her place in the world is granted.

The culmination of insecurity, mistrust, and fusion lays the basic foundation for narcissism. If a child does not feel safe enough to hazard emotional breathing room, significant aspects of her development stall. That early sense of being omnipotent, where others exist to take care of her without verbalization on her part, will remain intact. Reactions to praise and criticism are felt to the very core of her being; that sense of being fundamentally "wrong" will live in her implicit memory banks resurfacing when criticism is perceived. The caregivers will change faces, but the basic blueprint of her earliest relationship remains operative: separation is too threatening, distinguishing herself from another (her caregiver) too risky. This person ages with the core emotional wiring of a toddler. Her existence is confirmed when she is seen and applauded, shame experienced when criticized (or when she perceives criticism whether offered or not). Isolation and imagination are used for internal emotional repair, and her caregiver remains an extension of herself. This is a narcissist.

■ *Here is what gets embedded in childhood and creates problems later in life:*

- The caregiver, now partner, employer, friend, or lover, is viewed as an omnipotent presence, to take care of her without her even needing to speak her needs.

- She needs the caretaker to affirm her experience of the world. Without it, she fears she would cease to exist. For this person, the phrase "Without you, I'm nothing" is literally true.

- She maintains a perpetually vigilant awareness of her caregiver. This emotional tracking is required to be sure "I" (caregiver and child) am okay, here, together on the same page, safe in the world.

- She feels herself to be all good or all bad. She assumes others fit this template too.

- Praise makes her feel perfect and as if all is right in her world.

- Criticism is felt, and defended against, powerfully. Perception of slights will serve to maintain negative connection, and also provoke defensive reactions to create engagement.

- She attempts, in some sense, to control the current caregiver to have her needs met, get what she wants, and avoid separation.

- She feels very powerful and capable in her abilities and seeks recognition.

- She constantly attempts to please her caregiver in order to glean that attention and sense of safety and okay-ness that she craves. She watches and notes what seems to be success-ful, tallies those techniques in a developing rule book, and turns to them over and over.

- She becomes highly intuitive and relies heavily on pleasing behaviors when she has a potential new caregiver in her sights, or when she feels an established relationship might be threatened. In an established relationship, if she is not successful in her pleasing or placating tactics, she's likely to blame the other, feel she's a victim, and resort to anger.

- Her implicit memory holds that there is something funda-mentally un-worthy about her. She is "wrong" and unac-ceptable to the core.

- Physical proximity substitutes for emotional connection.

- Her all-important caregiver has the power to take away her sense of being acceptable and okay in the world through very simple shifts of attention.

- Negative attention will suffice as a tool for affirming her ex-istence, and will be provoked.

- She needs to be alone or aloof to cope with overwhelming feelings of shame and wrongness.

- In that aloneness she attempts to prop herself back up by retreating into the world where she's perfect and powerful.

Narcissism as Defined by the Psychology Profession

The tool used by professionals trying to decide if a person is a narcissist can be useful. Understanding what has transpired to create a narcissist helps make sense of the elements of the diagnosis. Be aware that this definition may change with the release of the next version of the DSM, expected in May 2013. The details of the diagnostic tool used within the psychological profession does not change the facts of the dynamics we describe in this book. These will continue to be useful to the reader no matter how the DSM handles narcissism.

The *Diagnostic and Statistical Manual of Mental Disorders* (DSM IV) currently uses this language to diagnose narcissism:

A pervasive pattern of grandiosity (in fantasy or behavior), need for admiration, and lack of empathy, beginning by early adulthood and present in a variety of contexts, as indicated by five (or more) of the following:

(1) Has a grandiose sense of self-importance (e.g., exaggerates achievements and talents, expects to be recognized as superior without commensurate achievements).

(2) Is preoccupied with fantasies of unlimited success, power, brilliance, beauty, or ideal love.

(3) Believes that he or she is "special" and unique and can only be understood by, or should associate with, other special or high-status people (or institutions).

(4) Requires excessive admiration.

(5) Has a sense of entitlement, i.e., unreasonable expectations of especially favorable treatment or automatic compliance with his or her expectations.

(6) Is interpersonally exploitative, i.e., takes advantage of others to achieve his or her own ends.

(7) Lacks empathy: is unwilling to recognize or identify with the

feelings and needs of others.

(8) Is often envious of others or believes that others are envious of him or her.

(9) Shows arrogant, haughty behaviors or attitudes.

Note: The language used is based on the *Diagnostic and Statistical Manual of Mental Disorders* (DSM IV-TR), Fourth Edition. Washington, DC: American Psychiatric Association, 2000.)

You will hear narcissism called Narcissistic Personality Disorder (NPD), pathological narcissism, unhealthy narcissism, covert narcissism, megalomania, egotism, self-absorption, or just narcissism. At the core, these terms all mean basically the same thing; an unhealthy self-centeredness, or self-absorption, combined with a futile search for sustained validation from others that impairs relationships.

In order for a person to be formally diagnosed as a narcissist, they are supposed to meet 5 of the 9 characteristics defined in the DSM-IV. A person who has 3 or 4 of the elements, but not 5, is known as a person with narcissistic traits or tendencies. This personality disorder is found in both men and women.

When 5 or more of the 9 criteria laid out in the DSM-IV are met, a person's personality has become rigidly defined by these characteristics. A professional would consider the behaviors to be "pathological," which means the narcissism is considered to be a disorder and exists to a degree that is extreme, excessive, or markedly abnormal. It leads to dysfunction in one or more areas of life, particularly in managing and maintaining personal relationships.

Narcissism Through the Life Span

It's not until a person is an adult that narcissism can be diagnosed. The groundwork is laid in early childhood, but can be influenced by so many factors and variables that the exact timing and process of its emergence is hard to generalize. Although a person can seem very narcissistic in adolescence, it's actually natural for every adolescent to go through a very "me" centered phase. It's a more sophisticated version of the two-year-old's process of separating from the caregiver, and the task is for the individual to lay the functional foundation necessary to support her as she goes out into the bigger world on her own. If a teenager is required to comply stringently to the requirements of parents she risks incorporating the message that it is not okay to be separate. She's also at risk for becoming very rebellious as a handy tool for creating separateness. It's incorrect to call a teen a narcissist, even though it might seem true. It's simply their job to do things their own way because they need to further establish themselves as separate and distinct from their primary caregiver and nuclear family.

In the twenties, narcissism may be hard to detect. The brain is still in development. The shining light of the soul can still be glimpsed. The feeling of connection may be possible. But as time progresses, and circumstances allow, narcissism can bloom into full being. This blooming will not happen on any specific timeframe, and will be expressed differently by different individuals.

In a narcissist's twenties and thirties she is likely to look good in her world. Her self-centeredness may not be very noticeable and is not likely to impair the natural development of relationships. A narcissist will assess the criteria required for approval from her chosen community and will strive to project the qualities of such a person. A narcissist's unconscious mind is a keen observer of what it takes to be liked and to succeed, and she will mold herself accordingly. Tons of training for this camouflage took place before she was three, in all that vigilant observing of the caregiver.

But narcissism can bloom into full flower if the circumstances are right. It's when she finds a particular companion who is good at caretaking, or conversely particularly dependent, or she develops an adoring circle of admirers. When the narcissist feels adequately adored and supported in having her needs met, she can relax and become fully herself. If there's not enough approval provided, a narcissist will move on, looking for the amount needed to quench her thirst. When she finds it, she will stay with that person or group even if it's not fully satisfying to her. If enough approval comes her way, and her comfort grows, she'll allow herself to be her true self. The dynamics described earlier will flourish. She'll invite people to interact with her as she needs, she'll unknowingly assume that others experience the world as she does, and she'll seek to impose her template of the world on others.

A young narcissist will repeatedly compare herself to other people, and will use these comparisons as motivation to make something of herself. She will seek to distinguish herself from other people, looking for ways to be noticed and recognized as better than the pack. She will tend to adapt the prevailing trappings of success in her particular world and not stick out as overly idiosyncratic (unless that's part of the trappings of success). She will adopt the values of the world she makes primary. Tendencies toward exclusivity will begin to show. These developments may not look a whole lot different from what everyone does in their twenties, healthy or unhealthy, but the undertone will be distinct. Self-doubt and self-judgment may be one of the more obvious markers, but it also may be kept masked or completely hidden.

Some narcissists move quickly from partner to partner. Others seem to fall deeply in love. The narcissist will use considerable charm to cast an enchanting spell over the person she finds romantically interesting. Her unconscious ability to ascertain the desires of another, a well-practiced skill learned with her caregiver, may craft her into the seemingly perfect partner. Although she will be incapable of true intimacy, she can create the impression of wanting it, experiencing it, and offering it.

As time passes in a particular relationship, she cannot sustain positive regard for someone close to her. Behaviors that seem like assumptions of superiority will start to emerge. Behaviors that seem like disrespect or disregard will come into play. She will be emotionally passive (responsive, though) and she will not seem particularly concerned with gratifying anyone other than herself. She will withdraw when she is overwhelmed.

Narcissism will get more pronounced over time. The basic framework is stable, but relationship trouble develops as life progresses and more people come into her orbit. She must keep adding pages to her rule book, and it gets increasingly complex to manage. She will not understand emotional nuance and will attempt to skate by, letting other people handle complex situations. People get frustrated or disappointed with her, and she struggles to understand and keep up. Her attempts to placate people may work for a while. She rejects people who no longer provide adequately for her.

For a while practice makes perfect and narcissism can be somewhat masked to the uninformed on the other side of a relationship with someone who is overly self-absorbed. The narcissist will have molded herself to succeed in the world of her choosing and will define herself as she thinks she ought in order to be recognized as a star in that world. As she finds success, she becomes more and more reliant on maintaining the image that makes her a success. She will treat people as having value only if they meet her needs.

People will be enticed into relationship with her without awareness of the dynamics likely to unfold. They will be seduced by her likability, by the shining glimpse of her soul, by her star quality, and may be hooked by her elusiveness. Commitments will be made—jobs offered, marriage proposals accepted. Over time, her relationships will become more clearly lacking in reciprocity. If she has found a work world in which she excels and is supported by people who are close but not too close, she can maintain high functionality in the larger world.

A narcissist will increase her boastfulness over time, seeking overt signs of approval. She will use deceit and outright lying if necessary to maintain claims of superiority, and to keep key people close. She may resort to disdain, denigration, hiding wrong doings, or violence against anyone she perceives as a threat to the structure of her world. The narcissist is unlikely to be aware of her own dishonesty. When her existence is threatened by separation, she will use whatever means necessary to remain joined. As a result, she becomes increasingly distant from the reality in which she lives with other people. She is likely to remember things differently than other people, and she rewrites experiences with her own particular spin, to suit her own purposes. Opinions that differ from hers can be perceived as threatening and can bring out behaviors with malicious outcomes.

As a narcissist ages, collateral relational damage will be left in her wake. Her inability to read emotional nuance will become apparent. Personal relationships will not last. Marriages will be rocky or end. New romances will be jumped into quickly, just as quickly ended. Jobs will not satisfy. Employers will not be happy. Business partnerships will be trying. Stability may be found if a narcissist takes up with another narcissist or with someone willing to be and remain entwined.

In the her 40s to 50s a narcissist's options may narrow— employers will be more picky and see trouble in past experiences, or may be less willing to put up with inappropriate social dynamics. Romantic partners are likely to have matured into self-confidence and be unwilling to nurture a narcissist long term. A narcissist sees reality differently than other people, and these gaps may become more obvious. The narcissist attempts to control her desired outcome, mostly by engaging with people she sees as wanting what she wants. The sameness of mutual desires makes relationships work. (Note: This is true of all relationships. It's called community or tribal affiliation from a healthy point of view.) However, at this age in human development, authenticity becomes highly prized by emotionally healthy individuals and it is difficult for the narcissist to comprehend or replicate. Her rules of engagement are compiled as a lumbering tome and sifting through the pages for reference to any given situation becomes ever more cumbersome as time progresses. This relational awkwardness increases with age, becoming ever more evident to potential partners or employers.

Current research seems to indicate that some personality disorders may be based in genetic predispositions, and that brain function may be affected or affecting the likelihood of a person to develop a personality disorder. Borderline personality disorder is one of these, and there seems to be some success in treating this disorder. Given our current level of knowledge, this does not seem to be the case for narcissism. Current consensus holds that narcissism develops due to dynamics of early childhood and that it is difficult to treat. Medications and therapy may be able to treat companion symptoms of narcissism, such as addiction or depression.

There is debate within the psychology community about whether or not an adult narcissist can individuate and discover another mode of relating. There is agreement that if it is possible it takes years of work. A narcissist usually will blow out of relationship with a therapist once the core issues begin to arise. The therapist/narcissist relationship requires a delicate dance and very light touch that can often go awry.

The foundation for narcissism is laid in the first few years of life, but does not become evident until adulthood. If you have discerned that you are in a work or personal relationship with a narcissist, awareness of the basics of how narcissism develops can help you have compassion for the narcissist and provide insight that allows you to better manage a relationship. It is all too easy and enticing to simply want to blame the narcissist for being the way she is and demand that she change. (Narcissists are very adept at eliciting this behavior since that is the stance of many caregivers in a narcissist's life.) Once you realize how deeply ingrained this problem is, how much it is part of the basic structure of this person's mind, you are more likely to see that your entreaties and efforts are likely to simply use your energy and not get results. If you have been persistent in seeking a satisfying personal relationship with a narcissist, you are probably angry, exhausted, and disappointed—all feelings you are tempted to direct at the person who you believe failed you. Understanding that this person is not choosing to do this to you, but would do this with anyone might help lessen your anger and give you more freedom in how you choose to interact as you go forward.

Chapter 3 | *Your Experience*

Although each narcissist expresses his personality individually, all narcissists share some ways of relating in common. So, while each of us relates to our narcissist as an individual, we all share some common responses and behaviors. This chapter explores how it feels to be on the receiving side of a narcissistic relationship. This may offer you a new perspective on your experience and a better understanding of whether the other person in your relationship is a narcissist or not.

Please be aware as you read this chapter, that when you are living with narcissism it can be very hard to identify. Reading this chapter, you might think, "It's so obvious! How did I not see this?!" But that is not how life is lived. It unfolds in a series of moments and experiences, and you are unlikely to have had the need to look at it in a big picture way until now. You are also unlikely to have had the information necessary to understand what was unfolding in your life. Please be gentle with yourself should this information provide insight to your situation. It is your seeking that has provided the revelations. There was no way to understand this schema before you went looking for answers.

The experience of being in relationship with a narcissist is not unlike the experience of being in the sun after being cooped up inside. At first it warms you, feels good on the skin, entices you to want more, even feels nourishing for the soul. You may notice that your skin changes color after a while, but you don't worry about it.

As time goes on, these effects continue, but you've gotten used to the heat and don't really notice. You're busy with other things anyway and it's not a big deal. After you've been in the

41

sun long enough, you begin feeling hot and itchy and tight. You may not be able to see the effects of exposure because you're still in bright light, but your sense of self-preservation kicks in and you retreat from the glaring rays. Only then do you see how red and parched your skin is. Suddenly, urgent care is required.

In this chapter we'll explore the predictable basic pattern of most narcissist's relationships, then we'll explore the various dynamics that tend to hook people into such a relationship, and finally, we'll explore common responses from those on the receiving side of the equation. We'll use the term "receiver" in this chapter, to refer to the person on the receiving end of a narcissistic relationship.

Common Patterns

A narcissist has a relatively stable internal system, and as a by-product, moves through relationships in a fairly predictable way, choosing partners already versed in these patterns or inviting the chosen to behave these ways.

It Feels Like a Good Fit at First

In the beginning everything seems so fine, even perfect, brilliant, in fact. You've encountered someone who understands you well—one with whom you feel aligned, down to the core. The welcome rays of the sun shine down on you.

Whether it is a friendship, a romantic or work relationship, there is something very attractive about this person. He has caught your attention, interest and appreciation. If you show positive regard, and there's something you have to offer a narcissist, then the narcissist begins the process of charming you into relationship. You probably won't notice how this person adapts to you in a chameleon-like way— you won't know that this person might be different with other people because you have only your own context and limited history together.

As a friend, a narcissist can initially be lots of fun. In the work world, the narcissist can be a star—accomplished, capable, making things happen. As a romantic partner, a narcissist at first feels like a perfect fit; you can be quite exhilarated and the relationship develops quickly. When a narcissist is attracted to you, the charm initially turned your way will be considerable and hard to resist. One woman called it "the narcissist's spell," and it is very much like that. Once you show interest, that interest is like honey to the narcissist and will be cultivated. The early stage is often fun, captivating, and enjoyable. He can feel like a very good mate, and nothing is more satisfying and exciting than that. Women frequently talk of thinking they'd actually met their "Prince Charming." Men talk of feeling as if they'd found their perfect match. He can be interesting, exciting, and witty. He is a carefree playmate and enchanting in a social setting. It is seductive to be the one on the arm of the star and the life of the party. It is delightful to be adored and admired.

It is in the work world that a narcissist is most quickly and easily unmasked; their attention-grabbing ways can raise eyebrows and create issues for other people.

Your reactions likely depend on the type of relationship that's developing. Your experience is generally less intense the less intimate the relationship.

■ *You are likely to feel:*

- impressed,
- pleased to have or get his attention,
- lucky to be the one with him, or working with him,
- special because of your affiliation with him,

- excited or energized in his presence,
- always wanting more, or
- proud.

In friendship, this person is impressive and interesting. Long-term consequences of your involvement are not particularly worrisome to you at this point. In working relationships, you probably have little choice about interacting and if you are hitting it off, you have no reason to suspect anything amiss.

If this is a romance, you are likely thrilled to have met such a fabulous match. In romance, you're swept off your feet with stars in your eyes. His persistence in pursuit is dazzling. Heavily influenced by the biochemical cocktail of infatuation, the critical thinking part of your mind is pre-occupied and is easily ignored. Conversation flows without your even noticing the scant interest he actually has in you or your viewpoint. His uncanny ability to tap into your deepest motivations is operating, but you are unaware of this.

The relationship can move to exclusivity so quickly that you may still simply be caught up in the excitement and the more slow moving, assessing part of your brain won't have time to notice or weigh in. Once a narcissist has you in his sights as a target of interest, he will maintain frequent contact and not allow much distance between you. Things can get heady and move in such a way that you may miss his superficial manner in inquiring about who you are.

This is particularly true if the narcissist is well-educated, well-informed, or an otherwise intriguing entertainer, conversant on a variety of topics. In a dating situation, his questions for you about you may not probe very deeply and anything beyond a perfunctory check-in is unlikely to surface much past the third date. But you may not even notice. It's not as if conversation suffers without that. A non-narcissist's habit of filling in any necessary gaps keeps conversation moving and induces the idea of your contribution. You may catch warning signs if you've already become educated about narcissism due to past experiences, but even then, unless you've become highly attuned, it can be easy to miss.

This initial stage where things feel great, and the warm rays of the sun feel nourishing, causes many on the receiving side to be willing to cement a relationship quickly. A narcissist tends to prefer this quick fix, so to speak, since the threat of being unveiled as flawed is nipping at his heels. The decision to make an investment in this person is made and once that happens, it is not readily questioned.

Kate remembers feeling starstruck in the beginning. She got involved with a man who was a key advisor in her educational program, and his graduate students were in awe of him. At a dinner with a group he ordered for everyone, and in a foreign language. Kate was more than impressed; at the time she also felt the warm glow of being taken care of.

You Feel Special

In the early phases of a relationship with a narcissist, you feel pretty special for being the chosen one. If it's a work relationship, you may feel lucky to be working together. If it's a personal relationship, you probably enjoy being the choice pick of this dynamic personality, and you also probably enjoy the attention that comes your way as a result of being his friend or companion. Narcissists are masters at appealing to a person's need to feel special. This can be especially enticing for people who like acknowledgment, but not too much attention, or for people who generally have been overlooked by others.

Julia remembers feeling both swept away and very special in the beginning of one of her relationships. He was likable, charming, attractive, accomplished, professionally respected, well off, and interested in . . . her. He shifted a professional relationship toward the personal by revealing details of his life that one would not normally share. He showed her his recently renovated home, and mentioned that the one room he had not re-done was intended to be the nursery, and he hoped the right woman would re-do that room with him. Within the initial month of dating, he introduced her to family members, and enquired if she'd like the city where he might move his business. She was smitten.

A Shift Occurs: The Fall from Grace

Invariably the relationship shifts after the glowing initial stage. We all expect a relationship to mature, and possibly even lose some of its luster. What we don't know is that in relationship with a narcissist there will be forms of trouble that are inevitable. Given the individual nature of each person, there is not a recipe for what problem will arise at any given time, but there are some common experiences you are likely to have.

With some narcissists this shift will be subtle, slow and hard to recognize or name, while with others it will happen overnight and be quite shocking. The shift may happen as soon as you are fully committed. It may happen as you assert more independence and aren't perceived as responsive or giving enough. It may happen when you experience some difficulty in your own life, or when you experience and express frustration at failing to find depth of emotional sophistication or support in the narcissist. Maybe it occurs after he's had enough positive feedback to feel comfortable truly being himself. It's possible that verbal or physical abuse will become part of the relationship dynamics; for some romantic relationships this starts the day after the wedding, for others it's more subtle and hard to distinguish.

A variety of behaviors will show up. Making plans together becomes frustrating unless you are highly agreeable or easygoing; you'll accommodate his schedule without reciprocity. He'll maneuver conversations toward himself, his accomplishments, and his interests. He'll jockey over control, either overtly or covertly. He may throw mild or major temper tantrums that lead you to avoid disagreeing with him, either by avoiding what upsets him or by avoiding him. He may employ threats. He may meet your anger with his own anger and keep issues between you from getting resolved. He may seem inconsiderate or disrespectful. He won't apologize easily and if he does, it's likely to feel forced or insincere. If there is a problem between you, he will mask it to others masterfully and will not bring it back up with you in order to reach resolution.

It's not necessarily easy to discern narcissism—it's more obvious in some than in others. The subtle ones are the hardest to identify; it can take a long time and many experiences for concern to surface and discovery to begin. Once past the initial spell-casting stage, issues do arise, but your investment and lack of awareness of narcissism may cause you to misidentify the cause of the troubles. You may attribute it to a natural maturation of a relationship, or as typical "guy" behavior, or as a "woman thing," or simply as the challenge of two people deepening their relationship. As experiences accrue you may get uncomfortable enough to look for information, to discover patterns and finally succumb to exhaustion from the whole thing.

Kate recalled a job offer she accepted from someone she later discovered was a narcissist. There were certain responsibilities she'd applied for, and a specific title attached to those duties. She was promised that none of it would be a problem. When she had moved to the new town and arrived at work, she discovered that the agreed upon title was not the one on her business card, and some of the promised projects were not forthcoming. The changes were not directly addressed, and when she questioned the situation, her "misunderstanding" was the convenient scapegoat.

Karen remembers the first sign of trouble with the accomplished man she dated. He'd invited her to a concert on a Friday night. The appointed time came and went and she wondered where he was, and why he was not picking her up as agreed. An hour after the concert had started he called (this was in the days before cell phones). He said he was calling from an airplane on the tarmac in the city he'd been in for a meeting earlier in the day, and that the plane had been grounded. He did not apologize for standing her up, he didn't explain why he hadn't called earlier, but rather appealed to how special she was that he was calling from the airplane.

Adaptation/Accommodation

It's totally natural to want your relationship to work and to do what you think it will take to make it work. Most of us who get involved and stay with narcissists are masters of adapting and we do so without being aware that we are adapting to problematic behavior; we are just doing what it takes to keep things smooth. Or it may change so quickly and drastically that you may be stunned and caught completely off guard.

Finding ways to adapt and make life work for you will be the hallmark of a relationship with a narcissist. You may learn to accommodate his needs, putting him first, minimizing un-pleasantness or disagreements. You'll become accustomed to him being the center of attention, shrinking in social situations to afford him the greatest spotlight; this keeps him happy. Your primary source of nourishment may be drawn from your work or life independent of this relationship. If you're accomplished at accommodating, you may fail to notice how your personal desires fade into the background as his take center stage. You are likely to learn to expect very little and to rely only on your-self to get things done. If the relationship is unsatisfying, you're likely to take responsibility and may think there is something wrong with your communication skills or with the way you are handling the relationship, or something wrong with you, and you'll try to make changes accordingly.

Without really even thinking about it, you may learn to avoid revealing yourself and your successes to the narcissist in your life, in order to be able to feel good about what you've accomplished without having it undermined. If it's a personal relationship, you may learn not to rely on him for emotional support. In an intimate relationship, you may find the sexual relationship flat and unsatisfying, that sense of intimate con-nection elusive. No matter which sort of relationship it is, you adapt in ways to make your life continue to work, without dis-agreeing too much or needing too much from the narcissist. A relationship can exist in this state for many years.

You Always Seem to Want More
Feeling empty after interacting with a narcissist is a common experience of the receiver. This is particularly true if the rela-tionship is a friendship or romance; it's not so much the case if it's a work relationship. However, you may come out of interac-tions feeling vaguely uncomfortable, or even drained.

Early in a personal relationship, you may easily disregard your own experience of wanting more because the feeling is vague and undefined, thus easily explained away. Spending time with a narcissist is a bit like eating cotton candy—it excites the palate, but is not nourishing or fulfilling. If you come away from time spent with the person in question feeling like you had fun but are somehow unsatisfied, not fully met, or just as if there was not enough substance there, it's worth noting. Or maybe you'll describe your experience as feeling blank or like you want to grasp for more or as if you had fun but didn't get your questions answered. If you observe closely, you may find you can't quite get his full attention, or that he has one eye elsewhere, or he answers the questions he wants to answer but not the one you asked, or something unspecified is just a bit off. This tends to bring up a motivation in the receiver to want to have more time with the narcissist, and to try again to get his attention fully and successfully.

In a family relationship, a receiver tends to have an underlying gnawing feeling of wanting "more" of him. You readily believe if he didn't travel so much, or work so much, or play golf so much, or whatever it is that keeps him away or distracted, your desire could be satisfied. You may argue for more time together, thinking that time will facilitate the connection you long for. Yet, if you are in relationship with a narcissist, regardless of how much time you spend together, you can never "get in" emotionally and what there is to receive can be off putting. No matter how much time you spend together, the feeling of being satiated remains elusive.

Several people married to different narcissists expressed how they would try to get their mate to stay home more often, in the hopes that being a unified team would emerge as a result. In hindsight, they were able to see they thought time together was the remedy for feeling disconnected, but that time together never solved the problem. Kate described years of trying to get more time with her husband. At first she tried to get him to travel less, and to work fewer hours. When he didn't, she quit her job believing more of her time and attention to the relationship would resolve the frustrated longing for more intimacy with her husband.

Frustration

Once you are solidly in relationship with a narcissist, discontent and annoyance emerge. During the early part of the relationship, you are easily enamored and find it easy and worth your while to adapt rather than insist on being met by the other person. Some narcissists charm a receiver into relationship and as soon as the commitment is made, change their behavior into something much less than charming. It's as if the perfect prince turns into a mean troll. This sort of dramatic personality change is certain to catch your attention and concern quickly. Even so, your disbelief can be so strong as to offer excuses and accommodation even then.

George had this classic experience. After dating for several months and being "head-over-heals" for this woman, believing she was the perfect partner and playmate, they married. The very next morning everything changed with no obvious cause. She was no longer the warm, welcoming companion he had dated. Rather, she was dissatisfied, disdainful, and demanding. He explained away her behavior as the stress of the wedding, a transitional adjustment of moving to his home when she was so attached to her own, and a stack of other accommodating excuses. It wasn't until after he was seriously injured at work and needed her assistance for recovery that he finally realized she was unable to provide the needed human resource. He did recover and shortly thereafter they divorced.

Frequently, though, problems accrue slowly, are easy to explain away, and aren't overly alarming. You are easily placated. If you are dealing with a subtle narcissist, you may be involved for a long time, slowly accruing experiences without really noticing how much you are adapting to his requirements. You deal with issues independently. Yet different problems arise from the same fundamental place. Your ability to get along and your investment in the relationship can carry you for a long time. As one receiver said, "I just accepted it. I conditioned myself for it."

▌ *Disheartening experiences common to those in relationships with narcissists:*

- Hassling over plans until you're content to continuously concede to his way.

- In a work situation, finding key people left out of the information loop, or kept from appropriate meetings. Undermining may be common.

- Weariness from repeatedly scheduling his social activities or responding for him to social requests. You may wonder how he maintains social contacts since he does not do much to initiate the work of maintaining his own relationships.

- Confusion or self-doubt when each of you recall vastly different particulars of the content or circumstances around an agreement.

- Dismay when he fails to tell you that he's no longer keeping an agreement.

- Unpleasant surprise and annoyance when he says one thing but does another if it suits him better at the time.

- Discounted or disregarded as he goes about doing his own thing, in his own way, and on his own schedule—oblivious to his impact on you or your schedule or on others who may be involved.

- Responsible for everything that, in his opinion, goes wrong. Disappointed if you hope for an acknowledgement or apology; should you get one, it may feel insincere.

- Feeling uninteresting or unimportant when he demonstrates little or no curiosity about you, your opinions, or your activities. You may feel alienated by his aloofness, and strive for his attention. When talking about yourself, you'll learn to speak quickly because his attention won't last long.

- Overlooked when he neglects to ask what you want. You may get tired of initiating conversations about what you want, or what will work. He may be willing to accommodate your preferences, but he doesn't initiate asking you what you want.

- Feeling misunderstood or ridiculed by his reaction when your wishes differ from his.

- Exasperated when he does things "for you" and you end up with something you didn't want in the first place; then, find yourself blamed when you are unhappy with what he has magnanimously provided for you.

- His indignation when you tell him what you want and he hears it as criticism; he labels you impossible to please or he calls you a nag.

- Embarrassment at his ingratiating behaviors toward others.

- Uncomfortable at the disdain he expresses for people.

- Tired from working hard to be "good enough".

- Rushed to clarify your intentions when he perceives your statements or questions as slights or insults.

- Devalued when he forgets important information about you or other seemingly important people in his life.

- Vexed when he fails to tell you important information that affects you or others.

- Finding yourself solely responsible for initiating discussion of emotional issues.

- Insulted by his critique of you.

- Indignant with his suggestions for your improvement.

- Distracted when he responds to your upset with his own upset, losing the thread of your original issue.

- Antagonized when you feel incomplete after a disagreement, yet find that he is content and proceeds as if the matter is resolved. This may be especially mystifying when the discussion is set aside simply due to having to be someplace else, but when you are alone together again, he seems to have forgotten all about it or finds it unnecessary to discuss anymore.

- Fading into the background at social gatherings as he monopolizes the conversation. Anxious about getting your own ideas into the conversation.

- Embarrassed that he contributes very little if the guest list doesn't meet his criteria of distinction.

If you see this list and recognize many of the feelings or behaviors, you may feel overwhelmed. But we don't operate in the world with a list of this sort in our minds. It's easy for us to write off many of these behaviors as temporary lapses, or communication failures, or typical male behavior, or work overload, or PMS or whatever current circumstances suggest.

It's surprisingly easy to disregard our own internal indications that something in our relationship is not quite right. However, when incidents occur repeatedly and daily over time, and when our personal resources have eroded, some of us begin to notice our own discomfort and start to wonder. We feel the heat of the sun on our skin and find it uncomfortable.

You May Look to Yourself as the Source of the Trouble

At first, the behaviors and emotional nuances listed above may seem fleeting and easily accommodated. It's over time, when the narcissist no longer needs to charm you into relationship and settles into reassuring routine, that dissatisfaction arises. Identifying why you're dissatisfied can be a challenge. Outward appearances may seem ideal. However, the emotional exchange you desire is elusive.

In these circumstances a receiver might grasp for answers through self-examination. If we change ourselves we can change the whole relationship. "Am I ungrateful, or unrealistic, or demanding, or bad, or lazy, or unable to love, or no longer 'in love,' or . . . ?" The list of theories we make up to explain our quandary can go on and on.

If you voice your doubts or questions about your own responsibility in the relationship, a narcissist is likely to support your self-doubt. How this plays out varies with the narcissist. One style is to be rather quiet in his agreement that you are flawed while another may become actively critical. The dynamic that unfolds adds to your confusion; your experience is full of contradictions and it's hard to know which ones to process and act upon. The narcissist can say one thing and do another, or say contradictory things, leaving the recipient unsure. If the style of the narcissist is to be rather subtle in his opinion that you are flawed, then you may go along for a while oblivious to the unfolding dynamic. If the narcissist is loud and clear in voicing his disdain, then you get the message, but may be unsure which message to believe—the one of respect or love, or the one of disrespect and disdain.

A narcissist will provide suggestions for improvement to a receiver. Depending on the narcissist's style these messages will be communicated subtly or loudly with a lot of clear direction. You may decide you want to improve the relationship by being different and behaving differently. You might change your look or get a new job or change in whatever way the narcissist thinks necessary. But if you are dealing with a narcissist, the results will always be dissatisfying. A receiver is usually not quite able to please a narcissist. If you make the requested changes, you'll find the finish line has moved and a new goal awaits. The experience is one of working hard in the relationship, but never quite getting it right, no matter how diligent your effort. Self-doubt is a natural by-product.

Trying to please a narcissist can be like trying to grab the brass ring off a merry-go-round.

Julia strives repeatedly to please her friend who is continually disappointed in her. That disappointment combined with her own loyalty and determination entices Julia to keep trying.

Emily has a family member who is always dismayed by the "failure" of other family members to be in touch or share information or handle their lives as he sees fit. No matter how hard they try, they never satisfy him.

Mark noticed that his communications don't get through, so he tried different ways of saying things. He tried to be more succinct, he aimed to give his wife all the information she might need (but didn't ask for) and even then, had trouble making plans with her for a date night. He thought that maybe he wasn't good at communication. He's worked on improving his communication skills, only to continue failing and consequently, he feels like a failure.

The common denominator among these three is their continued efforts to "get it right." Some felt inadequate and wanted to be enough, some felt dismissed and wanted to be "seen," some felt misunderstood and wanted to be acknowledged. None of these people gave up quickly or easily.

You May Feel Confused

Individual interactions can be flummoxing, and the overall nature of a relationship with a narcissist can be confusing. In relationship with a narcissist, daily interactions seem complex and aren't usually satisfactorily resolved. You learn to placate, accommodate, concede, or ignore. Basically, at some point, you get fundamentally frustrated. Unfamiliar with the system of dynamics at work, it's impossible to make sense of the relational process. When you do pay close attention, you may be surprised at what's been going on.

"Crazy-making" is a common term used by recipients in these relationships. You are likely to feel disbelief or disorientation from your natural style of relating due to your repeated interactions with a narcissist. There are many contradictions and they are hard to reconcile if you don't know the ways of narcissists' behavior.

■ *This book is full of descriptions of the dynamics that confuse a receiver. Here are just a few of them:*

- You count on him, only to be left in the lurch wondering what happened.

- You get blamed for screwing things up when it doesn't really seem like the mistake was yours.

- You trust what he says, but discover that his actions don't jibe with his words.

- You can't seem to get his support even though he is in a position to give it.

- When you're going through a rough time, instead of listening he undermines.

- You appreciate him, but it's never enough for him.

- You can't really tell—does he like/love you or not?

- It seems as though someone close to you should celebrate your successes in life, but he dismisses them or even becomes resentful when you succeed.

- He appears to be listening, yet he's rarely affected by what you say.

- The relationship seems very tight, yet not very close.

- You try to give him what he says he wants, but it doesn't seem to please him.

- No matter what you say or do, he perceives you as critical.

- When you are upset with him, he gets upset at you. Your issues don't get resolved, they just get shunted aside.

- In a committed relationship, the markers of love might be present—the words, the gifts, the monogamy, the family— yet it doesn't "feel" like love. The vulnerability required of love is repeatedly wounded.

- You conclude there's something wrong with you; you feel inadequate.

- You interact but don't experience acceptance. You feel unseen or missed.

❚ *These confusing messages go on and on. For example, in personal relationships, confusing questions arise:*

? Why didn't he book the tickets like he said he would?

? Why are you the one always expected to call, and he's offended if you don't, but he fails to phone you when he wants to talk?

? Why did he hear your compliment about his new suit as a remark about how lousy the old one was?

? Why did he bring home rocky road ice cream when you'd asked for chocolate? How come he can't remember your favorite kind is chocolate, anyway?

? How is it your fault that his computer was left in the trunk of the rental car at the airport?

? Why were you the one who was supposed to know that the movie started at 9 not 9:30?

? How are you supposed to handle that he's two hours late for a dinner party you've prepared for his business associates?

? Why does he blame you years later for a rough time you went through and tell you that you handled it badly and have never been any good since then?

? Why does he agree to decision after decision that create a certain kind of life and then tell you he never wanted it that way?

? Why did he want you to quit your job, and then blame you for quitting your job?

? How can he tell you you're a disappointment to him when he helped you make the very decision that is now cause for his blame?

? Why did he make it seem like finally finishing your degree was no big deal and attending the ceremony was an imposition, but when he finished organizing the garage it was cause for celebration?

? After years of thank-yous how can he tell you that you never say thank you?

? After cheering on his job changes and supporting him through his work challenges, how is it he can say you've never appreciated him or supported him?

■ *In the work world, here are some common questions that arise:*

? Why did he promise you a certain job only to give you a

different one once you start?

? How could he ask you to work on a big secret project, and ask someone else to do the same thing without telling you?

? How is it that he could change your responsibilities without discussing it with you in advance of the announcement?

? Why did you get left out of a series of meetings that are about your project?

? How could he agree to a certain budget only to present a different one to the board and then look at you in benign surprise when you question it?

? Why does he get angry so easily?

? Why does he seem so contemptuous so often?

▮ *If you're the boss . . .*

? Why does he not inform you of key developments?

? How is it that he alienates so many people he works with?

? Why is he unable to involve other important players?

? Why does he isolate and fail to communicate only to be indignantly surprised when confronted?

? Why does he feel entitled to more money when he knows things are tight?

? Why doesn't he support his team instead of blaming them when a mistake occurs?

? Why can't he adequately explain what is going on?

? Why do you hear one story line from him and a totally different one from other players?

Conflict

Conflict with a narcissist happens when your point of view or what you want differs from his perspective or desires. Depending on your style, the conflict can be so minor as to feel unimportant, or can be so big it leads quickly to violence. Conflict will be minor if you adapt or give in or develop an idea or solution in keeping with his point of view. Conflict will be larger if you hold your ground.

Emotions can escalate quickly unless the recipient moderates because a narcissist is unaware of the consequences of his behavior on the other person or the relationship. A narcissist will hold his ground and escalate in order to get his needs met. You'll either give in or give up or get out. In the beginning, a recipient doesn't realize how much conforming is required to keep the peace. It's natural for the recipient to attempt minimizing conflict and suppress the discord being experienced. Over time, it may become more tedious to give in all the time, and if you chose to stand up for yourself more often, conflict is the result.

In a work situation, these dynamics of inflexibility on the part of the narcissist concluding with accommodation or conflict may be evident earlier because the social dynamics of work are different than in the personal world. Remember—conflict can range from mild dissent to verbal abuse to violence. The lack of acknowledgment can be a hook to the recipient. You stay engaged attempting to be considered or have your experience validated.

Conflict may intensify when you are in a professional or personal quandary not involving the narcissist. Your diverted attention provokes a narcissist to bring the attention and focus back to him, so he may demand more at that time and add to the worries and issues you are trying to manage. At the least, you will experience the lack of support offered by a narcissist; perhaps he will do things that you ask of him, but he'll be unable to source useful ideas on his own. When you are in a difficult situation that does not have to do with him, you may actually be able to notice blankness in the support department, or you may get attacked while you're down.

With a narcissist, you will experience fights over the same petty issues over and over and over again. You may hear that you are a nag, or impossible to please but essentially it is the same conversation ad nauseam. Since the system of a narcissist is very stable and only changes for short periods of time, any lapse of predictability will be short-lived. This time period may be long enough to placate someone into staying in relationship, but not long enough to evolve an enduring or substantively different relationship.

Negotiation with a narcissist is largely a charade. You may be invited to engage in dialogue to share information, hoping to affect each other's points of view, but what actually happens is not necessarily what was discussed. As you observe, you'll hear a lot of talk and not see much change. A narcissist cannot put himself in another person's shoes. Considering the effect of his position upon others is out of his scope of perception.

Since a narcissist needs your attention to affirm his existence and have his needs met, he needs to do things to keep your attention. His tools are either to impress those important to him, therefore getting attention meant to make you proud, or to create conflict and get negative attention. No recipient can provide enough positive attention to a narcissist—it's like water off a duck's back, it rolls off rather than being absorbed. So a narcissist turns to provoking your ire—keeping you focused on him even though it feels bad to both of you.

John observed of his mate, "I realized it was an argument she was having AT me, not WITH me."

In a long-term close relationship with a narcissist, the receiver may resort to anger as a reliable tool to get the narcissist's attention. If you find that you used to be a joyful or contented person, but are now angry and grumpy most of the time, a long-term relationship with a narcissist may be the root. Anger can become your primary emotional tone. You are attempting every behavior possible to be seen, heard, and considered. People turn to anger, as an emotion powerfully felt in an attempt to be powerfully effective. Unfortunately, it's not.

Isolation

A narcissist takes care of himself by keeping interactions at a surface level and by minimizing contact with others. This dynamic plays out both in his social world and in his primary relationship. Socially, he may have many acquaintances, but no deep friendships. At home, he maintains contact with his significant other but is mostly emotionally passive, reactive, and aloof. It's possible to confuse this with introversion, in which a person recharges through time alone, but it's different in that the rejuvenating aspect is largely absent.

If you are in a long-term committed relationship with a narcissist, you too will experience isolation even if that is not your natural tendency when left to your own devices. A narcissist does not actively contribute to maintaining a social life, nor proactively assist when there are things to be handled for events with other people (unless told specifically what to do).

The partner, not the narcissist, ends up carrying most of the social load, and you can feel as if you're dragging your narcissist along much of the time. Most couples experience isolation when children come along. It's understandable to assume that this feeling of aloneness is common to all new parents and will subside as the children get more independent.

Flatness

The character of a long-term relationship with a narcissist develops into a bland existence spiced by conflict. You may think that there is something wrong with you that you can't feel the deep connection he claims to be offering. Spending time and effort to reclaim that once enchanting experience of closeness, is, unfortunately, ineffectual. With repetitious episodes of confusion and discontentment resulting from your efforts to influence, a numbing effect occurs. Rather than recognize the high cost of conflict as a means of excitement and instead of conceding powerlessness to effect change, the option to suppress the resulting discomfort is irresistible and builds a thicker and thicker wall of defense.

Emily expressed how life seemed to fade from black and white to gray after being in relationship with a narcissist for a while. Activities that seemed like they should be fun and facilitate connection just seemed to be one more thing to do. Their relating shifted into living two separate lives in one house, but with her taking care of all the details of home in addition to her work.

You May Find Yourself Distancing

Surprise in the face of a narcissist's behavior is common in the early phase of a relationship. Slight alarm at his telling you, without consultation, what you will or will not being doing, embarrassment at his unabashed comments in social settings, his immodest references to himself, and other small, excusable acts, accumulate over time. Even if you graciously accommodate, emotional distancing is predictable. If it's a work relationship, an extra layer of defense and a bit more space is warranted between you and someone who seems difficult or overly proud. Going along to get along or withdrawal and emotional distancing are self-defensive moves in these relationships. Protective stances can continue for years in an effort to preserve the relational ties. With enough practice the art of physical proximity and emotional distance is mastered.

Margo took to falling asleep on the couch in the living room, not realizing that she was seeking to avoid interacting at bedtime with her husband. She didn't realize that something was wrong, she just thought she was going through a late night phase. It was only later that she realized she was sidestepping engagements with her husband and structuring as much distance into their lives as she could without calling attention to it.

Sarah, married long term to her narcissist, crafted separate living quarters for herself and her husband so that she could avoid him as much as possible. Her life clicked along comfortably for her, except for when they needed to coordinate anything.

Exhaustion

If you are in a primary relationship with a narcissist that endures over a long period of time, it will, at some point, become exhausting. You may find your physical and emotional resources stretched beyond your capacity to manage well. Your body reacts negatively to the stress, and your self-esteem suffers. You may not even have any idea that your exhaustion, ill health, or stress stems from the close relationship with the narcissist in your life.

Exhaustion comes from routinely giving and not receiving sustenance in return. At some point, the experience of being thwarted in living a full life including a healthy give and take in love and connection just makes you worn out. Today's buzz is that if you don't feel loved it is because you are not open to love. Your worthiness is in doubt, a piece is missing from your childhood, or low self-esteem are all adequate barriers to bar love's reception. All this may be so, but when you are with a narcissist it is equally true that the reason you don't FEEL loved is that you are not. This one is hard to grasp when your beloved professes words of love, and many of the markers of "love" seem to be present. However, it's easy to wear out and succumb to exhaustion if you keep chasing the enticing carrot of actually experiencing the emotional connection professed so beautifully by the narcissist.

You Become the Enemy

If you decide that you are seriously dissatisfied with your relationship and you express this dissatisfaction, you should be prepared to become the narcissist's instant enemy. Your attempts to change the nature of your relationship, will be experienced as threats by a narcissist. Even your voicing of thoughts about ending your relationship is, for the narcissist, the ultimate rejection. It exposes the narcissist's deep vulnerability. A narcissist will feel humiliated and threatened. Whereas in the beginning, you were "all good," now you are "all bad." A narcissist faced with this situation might say he is willing to work on things, and he might even attempt to do so, but he is not likely to follow through on these changes. Your search for connection and your attempts at change will be met with anger, threats, manipulation and sometimes even violence.

Quick Replacement

If you end a primary relationship with a narcissist, you are likely to be replaced very quickly. If you chose to stop adoring, accommodating, and care-taking a narcissist, his need for a reliable anchor of reflection will propel him to find someone else willing to provide this service for him. Serial marriages are common for people with this issue. Narcissists do not know how to be in the world without being fused with another person as the navigator and emotional linchpin. For most narcissists, being alone is equivalent to being obliterated; they don't know how to define themselves unless they are reacting to, or aligned with, another person.

Common Hooks

Narcissists have an incredible unconscious ability to offer irresistible invitation to relationship. They have learned through painful experience what it takes to procure an adoring gaze. It's uncanny how savvy a narcissist can be at exploiting an opening—frequently openings that receivers have no awareness of offering. And, it's not just that the beckoning is offered and accepted, it's that the hook created by the narcissist sinks deeply and effectively into the receiver without anyone's conscious awareness.

Emotionally healthy people assume that they are participating in an openhearted exchange with commonly held groundrules of human relating. Regrettably, this is not so. You know you exist as an autonomous human being. However, he knows only that your existence verifies his own. This fundamental difference is not overt nor evident for some time. If you are the object of interest to a narcissist, you are likely to become enmeshed before you even know it. The ways in which a narcissist appeals to a non-narcissist and impounds the relationship are probably too many to describe but it's worth naming at least a few, highlighting how easy it is to fall prey to them.

Specialness: A narcissist can make a person feel incredibly special. He effortlessly appeals to your desire to be known and to know. His attention makes you a star because he is a star that admires you. He will blatantly applaud your intelligence, attractiveness, or creativity—whatever quality he senses carries the most vulnerability for you. What's not to like about finding yourself so highly regarded, so ardently courted, so deftly pursued. If it's a romance, he will tell you how much better you are than the last person he was with and will paint a pretty picture of a possible future. Narcissists are masters at appealing to a person's need to feel special.

In return, he expects you to do the same. It may not be too difficult in the beginning, so things can go swimmingly for a while. Over time, this issue of specialness may continue to hook you, but in a different way—you will chase the brass ring of trying to continue to be admired by him, even as you fruitlessly try to make him feel as special as he needs to feel. The initial stage of the relationship is like a training ground where his expectations are set—and this is exactly what he wants in return. He wants you to make him feel this special, too. This is his training field where he establishes the unreasonable criteria that you must meet to make him feel special . . . criteria so unreasonable that you can never meet them to his satisfaction.

Youthful Naivety: There are so many things a young person does not know and can only learn through his or her own painful experiments. The wisest adult is unlikely to be able to keep a young person away from dangerous exposure. A youthful narcissist can be very hard to discern—they are emerging from the stage of appropriate teenage narcissism. They haven't had adequate time at trial and error, revealing and mastering their behavior patterns. Testing relationships and changing jobs is age appropriate and may not indicate a possible personality disorder. A narcissist may offer shining glimpses of their soul, enticing a young person into relationship. Naivety and optimism can draw a person in unwittingly.

Hope: Once you commit to the relationship, it is hard to give up hope that it will work. This hook of hope is the basis of everything else that keeps drawing you in and keeps you involved. Relinquishing hope to the reality of the relationship is particularly difficult for persistent, strong-minded people. An independent fortitude is very attractive to narcissists because it means the receiver is convinced the relationship can work, if only you put enough effort into it.

Trying to Reclaim that Sense of Specialness: A person who experiences that sense of specialness in the initial stage of the relationship will know it's possible to feel that and can be enticed into constantly seeking to experience that again.

Wanting to Be Respected: Once a person is hooked, a non-narcissist may maintain the relationship simply in an attempt to be recognized, respected, considered, or seen. In an attempt to accommodate, you may even move past your desire to feel special and admired, and settle for simply wanting to be acknowledged and considered. The receiver usually is not aware that this simple human need for respect is being thwarted. But by being unaware of the "rules" of this relationship you can be hooked into chasing the carrot of respect and recognition, not realizing this is a carrot you can never attain.

Attempts to Get it Right: Again, past the initial charming stage, a non-narcissist may stay in relationship simply to recover that initial sense of delightful perfection: a keen alignment between the two of you wherein you were met and known—or, at least, thought you were known. You will try saying it this way, or doing it that way, all in vain attempts to be *gotten*. This can keep a non-narcissist busy in creative ways for years, pushing to obtain the unobtainable.

Trying to Get His Attention: Simply getting a narcissist's attention in order to experience the fundamentals of a good relationship puts you, the non-narcissist, on a never-ending treadmill of activity. You seek that experience of being well matched and suited for one another that you knew in the beginning. Since it's your historical experience, you think it's possible to reclaim that. You may go to all sorts of lengths to get that essential attention again. You hope that more time together will do the trick, or you imagine having a better body will bring you closer to him, or in anger you resort to many other tactics all revolving around trying to be seen or known and feeling connected.

Caretaking: A narcissist might appeal to your inner caretaker. He will have personal issues that are obvious to you (self-doubt, troubled relationships, lack of recognition, addiction, suicidal thoughts) and you may put your relationship needs aside to care for the needs of the narcissist.

Chasing Confusion: Some of us hate to be mystified. Confusion presents us with a puzzle to be solved, an intellectual problem to be conquered and we will not rest till we understand. Things that do not make sense are not taken as a warning, or as a sign of trouble but instead as something new to be figured out and handled. Some people have the tenacity to try to unravel every confounding element in their relationship. They "work on it." As Mark confessed, "I just couldn't accept that it was possible for it to be this way. I had to stay to prove it wasn't true."

Fear: A narcissist uses threats to keep people in line. The threats may be veiled so that you don't even take them as threats; "I love you so much that if you ever leave me, don't know what I'd do." If a person is highly conflict averse it can be easy for a narcissist to keep them in line—slight hints of discontent on the part of the narcissist motivate instant accommodation. If you don't mind some conflict, then you can expect the narcissist to push back. There may be emotional, financial or physical coercion, manipulation, intimidation, and the like. Because these behaviors are disquieting, even frightening and because these behaviors feel so ominous, most people learn to avoid such encounters, especially after tangling a time or two.

Conflict and Drama: Some people feel alive and connected when there is conflict and drama in their lives. Even non-narcissists may mistake the intense closeness of drama as a sign of love. A person with a family history of high emotions will feel at home with a narcissist.

Commitment: That legal document, whether it is a business partnership or a marriage license, is taken very seriously by most of us. The vow of "Til death do us part" is pledged in earnest and signifies our intention to do what it takes to make it so. Children add a dynamic of commitment not just to marriage but to family. Changing these commitments can be difficult beyond words.

Common Responses

When you live with a narcissist in your life, whether it's a parent, a mate, or colleague, you will adopt coping mechanisms. When you've been in the sun too long, you need to protect yourself— you don a hat, look for some shade, move out of the hottest rays. Just so, when you become uncomfortable or blistered by your relationship, you make attempts to protect yourself. What follows is an alphabetical list of common attempts:

Accommodation/Adaptation: Narcissists get their way, and for some of us it's not that big a deal to let them have it. This is particularly true for receivers who value having a smooth relationship over having their way. Over time, however, accommodation gets increasingly hard to sustain.

People are taught that relationships take compromise, and so we adapt. Early in the relationship, it can seem pretty easy to accept the other person's needs. Through experience, you learn to avoid the sore spots and over time you navigate around them without even knowing you are doing so. Remember the experience of being in the sun—at first it feels good, you acclimate to the warmer temperature, but as time goes on you notice it feels too hot, too uncomfortable. Then, at some point it becomes unbearable and you seek relief. With a narcissist, you can be very happy at first, willing and able to accommodate, but as time goes on and trying experiences accumulate, your graciousness declines. It's especially difficult to maintain once you notice that you are the only one supporting and nourishing the union.

It is possible to become completely exhausted when you're in a close relationship with a narcissist—the level of depletion can be so deep as to leave you feeling on the edge of an emotional or physical breakdown. When you have absolutely nothing left to give, you are likely to want to get out or at least change things to find relief.

Anger: Because your personhood is not recognized, anger flash points are common occurrences when dealing with a narcissist. At some point, you may get so totally fed up that anger becomes your primary mode of expression with the narcissist in your life. It may be that anger is your way of standing up to him, your attempt to get his attention, your way of expressing your distress in the relationship. It may be that anger is your means to get space for yourself. As a receiver if you still feel disconnected despite your efforts, you may resort to anger as a way to affirm and feel your own power as an individual rather as an alternative to the ineffectiveness of trying to please a narcissist.

Emily described developing an angry undertone when dealing with her mate. She'd been in relationship for many years, without realizing how passive her husband was in their relationship. Over time, she was worn out but didn't know why. Her patience ran out along with her energy, and she became irritable. At some point, she recognized how unhappy she was in the marriage, and she began using anger as a means to get her husband's attention since all her other tactics had failed.

Attempts to Change the Narcissist: People who think they can change another will be kept busy identifying improvements for anyone, including a narcissist. Engaging in this can result in years of frustrating distraction. Those who believe they are dealing with communication problems, or a lack of relationship skills, or simply typical "stuff"—dynamics that might be improved by talking, or a workshop, or therapy, or couples counseling—have more dismay in store. A narcissist is unlikely to think there's anything wrong with himself that needs changing, but he might go to therapy if he thinks he can "help" his mate change. A narcissist tends to present a stance of benevolence toward those close to him; an attitude of "I'll do what you want if it helps you." The act is one of seeming self-sacrifice, but it's actually self-serving.

Young women seem to fall more commonly into this trap and spend years unaware of what they are doing. They see the potential in a man, rather than accepting him for who he is and deciding if it's a fit for them or not. It's a recipe for woe rather than a successful relationship, but if she's fallen for a narcissist, he'll thrive due to the attention and conflict the change project generates.

Attempts to Change Yourself: Individuals involved with narcissists get seduced into thinking there is something wrong with them or the way they do things. If only they could get it right, they would feel the respect or love being professed by the narcissist. Even an emotionally healthy person can harbor unrecognized self-doubts and end up locked in frustrating interchanges with a narcissist. A narcissist capitalizes on the other person's self-doubts. Because he is so familiar with self-doubt himself, he readily spots uncertainty and immediately reinforces any hint that there is something wrong with you, or something insufficient about you.

Eventually, a receiver will become critical, angry, and hard to please or subservient. Because fundamental exchanges are unsatisfying and confusing, and because the receiver is constantly invited into conflict, many receivers experience profound changes in their own behavior and personality. These are not initiated with self-awareness, rather they are reactions of self-preservation.

Laura was married to a narcissist and found herself being very critical while they were together. For years after they split up she worried about her behavior: what was wrong with her that she could be so crabby to the man she loved? She guarded against being critical and monitored herself in every subsequent relationship, worrying that the critic inside would rear her ugly head when least expected. She had no idea that she had adopted that behavior in response to the needs of her narcissistic spouse.

Avoidance: You learn how to avoid conflict and the resulting dismay by giving in, or shying away from interaction. Such evasion keeps the narcissist central to your actions since he is the one you seek to sidestep. A recipient in a long-term relationship overlooks personal desires while navigating her distance from the narcissist.

Dependence: You concede to the narcissist's controlling structure. Choosing this option obliges you constantly to seek the unattainable acknowledgment and approval from an ever-moving target. If you've ever known independence, you cannot forget it; maintaining a position of subjugation will be impossible to sustain over time. Suppressing your need for autonomy is possible for short periods, but not the long haul.

Depression: A person deeply involved with a narcissist is a candidate for depression. Living closely with narcissism requires one's creative energy to be focused on another person without nourishing reciprocity. Holding this focal point requires a great deal of stamina. Vitality for personal endeavors is depleted. Without some source of sustenance, life drains out without refreshment. One man involved long term with a narcissist described his depression as a form of oppression. "You keep settling, giving up ground."

Disappointment: Frequent and repeated disappointment wears on the relationship. You may feel disappointed in the other person for behaving the way he does. You may feel disappointed in yourself for getting into this situation or for letting it continue as long as it has. You may feel disappointed in yourself for failing to "succeed" in adapting enough or failing to change or enlighten the narcissist in your life. Whatever the source, disappointment fundamentally changes you.

Erosion of Self: The closer and longer the relationship, the more you lose your own sense of self. You forget who you are at a fundamental level. Personal needs are overshadowed by the needs of the narcissist or by the need to keep the pitching seas calm. Adaptation, avoidance, and anger join together to erode your own authenticity.

Erosion of Self-Confidence: Even a confident person will find themselves uncertain during episodes with a narcissist. Having your self-confidence diminished is the natural consequence of long-term relating to a narcissist. Unable to comprehend a different point of view or an idea disparate from his own, a receiver is compelled to embrace, or at the least entertain, the interpretation of events or behavior of the narcissist. Doing otherwise leaves the receiver feeling stupid or wrong. It's impossible to maintain a relationship with a narcissist without granting unconscious agreement with his message of your being somehow flawed. To dispute this leads to conflict. If you persist in your belief in yourself, you must limit yourself in the company of the narcissist or excuse yourself altogether from the relationship.

Exhaustion: Eventually, many people in long-term relationships with narcissists get worn out physically and/or emotionally. Tapped out, they have nothing left to give. This is a perfect setting for stress-related physical symptoms to arise, sometimes severe or life threatening.

Hopefulness: We want to be successful in relating to others. When dealing with a narcissist it is a tough road after that early glittering stage. Some people don't even notice the shift, while others notice but can't figure out the problem. If it's a romantic relationship, many people expect some change when the initial "in love" feeling of infatuation wears off and so assume this is natural. If it's a less intimate relationship, you might notice something is a bit different but not be attuned to it, and again, won't think of the shift as anything to worry about. If you've chosen to be in a relationship, it's reasonable to hope it will work. If it's not satisfying enough you may hold to the notion that change is possible, or seek signs that improvement can happen. Some of us may be eternally hopeful that we will be able to change, or the narcissist will change enough that relating can become good, that the emotional underwriting will pay off. If you've embarked on a business partnership, or marriage, or started a family, you have an investment in that relationship, and you do what it takes to make it work until you can do it no longer.

Feelings of Being Ineffective/Inadequate: Whether working on a project with a narcissist or in a long-term relationship with one, feeling ineffective is common, unless you agree with him. You may feel futility at communicating, or persuading, or negotiating. Basically, you'll feel ineffectual at getting your point across. You won't be taken seriously. This will affect each receiver differently; some will trigger immediately; they will get into a conflict. Others may not notice the dynamic and will keep trying different tactics to be considered. In a less dedicated, short-term situation a triggered receiver is likely to walk away from relating, if possible. In committed relationships (whether work or personal), it's not so easy to walk away and a receiver will struggle over how to deal with a narcissist.

Isolation: In a committed relationship with a narcissist, you will experience isolation even if you are naturally gregarious. Emotionally, the narcissist is not engaged with you and isolates himself when upset to handle his issues. You'll feel isolated and disengaged due to his aloofness. Socially, he either prefers to minimize his contact with people outside of work obligations, or he wants things his way and is not very flexible or supportive. A narcissist can both charm and alienate people. If he alienates people in your social circle, invitations diminish. You can feel as though you're dragging all the weight of your mutual social life by yourself. After a while, it's probably not worth it to you and you slowly give up activities or friends.

Isolation can seem as if it's just a natural part of life's unfolding—you're part of a couple now, or children come along. It's understandable to assume that this feeling of aloneness is common to all new parents and will subside as the children become more independent. Yet, even if you maintain a strong social network, you're likely to be isolated from it and feel isolated within it.

If the relationship is a marriage, isolation is fed by our cultural tendency to keep marriage problems private. This is a logical and compassionate behavior in most cases, but with a narcissist it can keep us from having important reality checks, and keep us from getting support that could be useful. On the other hand, it might protect us from people who do not understand, or who unwittingly give poor advice.

When married to a narcissist you may find yourself guarded and withdrawn from the friends in your life, even the close ones—you're simply unlikely to share with anyone (maybe even yourself) the extent of the difficulties you deal with on a daily basis. If you do start to understand and discuss it, you're likely to be met with surprise and disbelief (if your narcissist presents well to the outside world and hasn't alienated people), which can lead to your feeling even more confused and alienated.

Julie, an extrovert, found herself subduing her outgoing personality at parties. She noticed that if her husband was not in the room she was easily included in conversation, but when he was around she shrank her energy, kept her jokes quiet, and deflected attention from herself.

John learned to enjoy his successes quietly. If he shared them with his girlfriend, she hardly acknowledged them or she belittled him in some way.

Repression: In order to maintain a difficult relationship, many of us simply figure out how to go along to get along. We get accustomed to the behaviors of narcissism and may not see anything wrong or particularly unusual in how we have revised our engagement styles. Some of us may even interpret a narcissist's behaviors as signs of love. We repress all sorts of things—desensitizing ourselves to our own desires, temporarily adapting our personalities, quashing our anger or frustration. Some of us develop an awareness that something is not quite right, but for our own reasons find it easier or better to avoid looking too deeply so we can evade the implications.

Minimization of Self: The limelight keeps a narcissist calm. Distracting from his brilliance by sharing your personal successes leads to problems. He will compete to regain center stage, discounting or undermining your accolades. You'll avoid sharing your own success in order to avoid having it discounted or having it become a problem.

Resentment: Feeling indignant or unhappy due to some behavior or remark from the narcissist is typical. Resentment is likely to pop up both as reaction to singular events, and as a common practice throughout your relationship with a narcissist. Resentment is often coupled with self-pity.

Self-Sufficiency: Some of us respond to the whole conundrum of dealing with a narcissist by becoming incredibly good at taking care of ourselves, without needing or expecting much from the narcissist. This sort of person handles things in an opposite manner from someone who turns toward dependency. You learn that the narcissist is not dependable, so you bypass all his unreliability as much as possible and set up your life to operate smoothly, needing little from him, even if he's your co-worker or spouse. In an intimate relationship, you may go so far as to have your own separate social life, your own income, pay the bills, and manage the house while figuring out the simple things a narcissist can and is willing to handle and without messing you up too much if he fails. A marriage of this sort develops into one of companionship but not partnership, it becomes two parallel lives that run next to each other, yet rarely intersect.

Tenacity: A person determined to make a relationship work can and will try all sorts of things. Tenacity combined with hopefulness can keep a relationship going for a long time. The drive to be seen and connect is very fundamental in a human. An uninformed person can tenaciously stay engaged in trying to be seen, respected, and considered until they wear themselves out.

Withdrawal: Withdrawal is a tactic, sometimes coupled with successful self-sufficiency. This involves constricting your emotional bond with the narcissist, while going through the motions of relating—visiting his reality while quietly maintaining your own, different perspective without drawing too much attention to yourself or needing very much from the narcissist in your life.

Getting and staying involved with a narcissist can be an intense personal experience. In the beginning, there is not much to warn you of what is to come down the road. Charm lures you into relationship and diverts your attention away from little things that signal warnings. Once you are committed, whether it is in a work situation or personal relationship, you are hooked into doing what it takes to make the relationship run smoothly. This leads you to explore tactics and strategies that smooth out the many rough spots and preserve your self. Your words may be different from the ones used here, and your own experiences may be slightly different from the stories shared here, but if you recognize these patterns, it will be worth your while to heed what is happening. Protecting yourself from the rays of the sun, in whatever way works best for you, is wise.

"Most problems you experience with a narcissist hark back to the fact that in his or her unconscious conception of the world, he or she does not know that you exist as an individual."

Chapter 4 | *The Fundamentals of a Narcissist in Any Relationship*

Having focused on what narcissism is, how it develops and common reactions to it, we will now turn to a deeper examination of the dynamics of the relationship between the narcissist and other people. Narcissism includes specific behaviors that can be recognized and understood. Clarifying what is going on with the narcissist and why these things happen can build a base from which you can make informed decisions about your relationship.

The mental map of an adult narcissist is that of a fragmented self, codified in neural networks that get reinforced over time as the same patterns run in the brain again and again. A narcissist remains unconsciously enmeshed with the significant people in her life. She is so much a part of that other person that her unconscious mind experiences that person as part of herself, an extension of herself who is there simply to meet her needs. A person lacking a whole separate sense of self is not free to move back and forth between separation and unity. It takes a whole, separate being to be able to appreciate and enjoy another whole, separate being. This dynamic is in play not only with a romantic partner, but also with the other people she incorporates into her world. She scans her environment seeking people open to her with whom she can exercise the only way of being she knows.

Primary Relationships versus Secondary Relationships

A primary relationship is one of major significance in your day-to-day life. Usually this sort has or had continuous physical proximity and some form of commitment. Family members or business partners can be primary. A parent you no longer live with is a primary relationship—one in which even small comments hit hard. A spouse is primary, as is a best friend. A former spouse may be primary if you are still co-parenting. A sibling may or may not be primary for you at this point in your life. A boss may be primary.

A secondary relationship is one where there may be some level of commitment or imposed engagement but with more space. This could be a colleague, employee, a project collaborator, or a friend. It's someone you interact with, who impacts you, but who is not consistently in your space or of major impact on you day to day for long periods of time. It's marked by either ongoing involvement with infrequent contact or intense involvement for a specific period of time.

The narcissist relies upon a primary relationship for sustenance. Secondary relationships provide some level of this as well, but to a lesser extent. (Think of these secondary relationships as vacation spots visited by the narcissist).

A relationship that develops fast and becomes permanent quickly offers dynamics that can be hard to unmask. Problems show themselves over time and through repeated experience. Commitment, optimism, and hope can grease the wheels for quite awhile. (Though this might not be the case if disagreements arise early in a relationship and the non-narcissist holds her ground.)

Oddly, it may be easier for you to recognize narcissism in a secondary relationship than in a primary one. When you are enmeshed (in a primary relationship), it is sometimes impossible to see the forest for the trees. A narcissist tends to be charismatic, but ironically not so good at dealing with people. This can sometimes be more apparent in secondary relationships, such as work or other social settings where the stakes are lower and there is more space between people (and possibly less tolerance for awkward behavior).

In a secondary relationship, the decline of the relationship may be slower and less apparent to both parties because it's only a visiting place, not a dwelling. The receiver has less time with the narcissist, fewer incredible interactions, and more time to recover and heal. Also, the receiver gets sustenance from other sources, and so is less reliant upon the narcissist for emotional exchange.

What follows is a description of the basic inner workings of a narcissist in any relationship.

Unaware of Others, She Lacks Empathy: Fundamentally unaware that other people exist separately from her and have their own needs, she doesn't inquire about the desires of others and isn't motivated to give them what they want. She doesn't consider things from another person's point of view. The absence of empathy impairs her ability to relate meaningfully with others. She requires emotional leadership from those around her. She doesn't understand you.

The Reality of the Narcissist Is the Only Reality: Her lack of an independent self is not apparent to her or to those with whom she gets involved. She unconsciously re-creates her original primary relationship in all her subsequent relationships. She searches for partners with whom she can mesh and create a form of connection that is very different from the connection between two people with a healthy, whole sense of self.

Poor Listening and Questioning Skills: Unaware that there is a reality outside of her own, her interest in the internal world of others is limited. Her curiosity is not deep, unless the information is of use to her for her own purposes. This means that observation skills, question asking, and listening are limited. One or two questions may be the extent of it. One or two word answers may satisfy in response. Female narcissists may be socialized to ask more questions, but again, the depth of interest will be lacking and so deep listening and understanding are vacant.

Unreliable: Since a narcissist does not register other people, she does not feel responsible to them. She does what she wants when she wants. She neglects agreements, she can't anticipate another person's wants or needs, and she's likely to forget another person's requests. In short, she cannot be relied upon in personal situations.

Broken Agreements: A narcissist will say one thing and do another, with no remorse. In the moment, she is attempting to please the person with whom she's interacting, attempting to look good, attempting to maintain approval. Later, she may not even remember her commitment. If she does remember it but it no longer suits her, she'll do what she wants without it occurring to her that she might have a responsibility to let the other person know what's going on. She is unlikely to apologize for this because she truly thinks she did nothing wrong. If there is an apology it is likely to be of the "I didn't do it on purpose" sort.

A Narcissist Is Always Right: Blameless, Blameful, and Without Apology: The narcissist perceives herself as the only one who matters. Because she's unaware that others exist, she takes for granted that others are extensions of her. Hence, what she wants and does is right in her mind, and any protests made to the contrary are essentially invisible and immaterial to her. Her way is the only way because she's the only one. Additionally, she is living from a rule book and furiously scrambling to maintain control. In her conception of the world, each situation has a prescribed set of responses that are supposed to work. If they do not work (they tend to fail as life gets more complicated), then it is not her fault—to her, she did it right. If things don't work out, she's sure it is someone else's fault, someone else's wrongdoing, or someone else's shortcoming. She takes credit when things go right and places blame when things go wrong. Problems are either ignored or reduced to figuring out who is at fault (and it's never the narcissist). If there is an issue to resolve, she will not be able to come up with adequate solutions because she is not capable of understanding that she may have some responsibility for creating the problem.

What Seems Like Superiority or Disrespect: The narcissist seems inconsiderate, disrespectful, rude. However, this lack of respect comes from a profound lack of awareness that you even exist as a distinct, separate individual; the narcissist doesn't realize that you are a person who has needs that deserve respect. To be respectful of another person requires that one is first aware of you. Lack of consideration implies that the other person is aware of you and your needs and makes a decision to do as she pleases while ignoring your preferences—which is not what happens with a narcissist. Emotionally healthy people, who operate with an awareness of others, who take others into consideration as a matter of course, have a very hard time understanding that the narcissist doesn't. You have a hard time grasping that a narcissist isn't intentionally selfish or inconsiderate; that she truly doesn't realize that there is anyone to consider other than herself. You are simply part of her personal equation, not separate from it. Her conscious mind may think she respects you, and may tell you she respects you (because that is the language other people use and she thinks she's the same); yet she has no concept of respect and consideration because her frame of reference is exclusive to herself.

A Narcissist Will Express That She's Been Mistreated: Along with blaming others for difficulties, the narcissist will feel put upon by all the trouble. She will unknowingly set herself up for difficulty, then feel as if she's the victim, the innocent, the martyr—the displeased, demanding, complaining, nagging, arguing other is the cause of the troubles.

Emotionally Unaware of Herself: A narcissist lacks emotional self-awareness. She will not have words to correctly identify her own emotional state. She will not have the tools to address her own emotional needs. She will wait for someone else to identify emotions and address emotionally charged situations, or she will use her limited repertoire of responses to get the attention focused back on her. She might in fact develop the language of emotional intelligence as she gleans rules from her experiences. However, her facility with authentic emotion will remain limited.

Evaluating her own emotional nuances is beyond her scope, but she will adopt the observations of others as they suggest emotional states. She will acknowledge that she is "angry" but only after someone else has pointed it out or reacted to her angrily. She rarely volunteers emotional assessments of herself in conversation until another person makes a fitting observation. Hijacking (or taking on) the emotional state of another person, and claiming it as her own, is commonplace.

Emotional Learning Does Not Get Internalized: When disagreements arise in relationships between non-narcissists, agreements will be made, tacitly or verbally, about how to resolve the problem and, hopefully, avoid a similar problem in the future. People don't always remember their commitments, and revert back to old habits, but generally, learning to coexist peacefully is internalized. This is elementary to getting along with each other and minimizing upset. In relationship with a narcissist, conflicts arise, resolutions are proffered by the non-narcissist partner, agreements about how to handle things in the future are made, the narcissist adds this to her set of rules, and then, within about two weeks she usually forgets all about the agreement and reverts back to habitual ways of being. The rule "remember this" seems perpetually absent in her book of proper behaviors.

Unable to Manage Her Emotions, Others Serve as Caretakers: Her tools for navigating her own emotions, the emotional state of others, and appropriate behavior, are limited. As a toddler, she expressed her emotions bodily and people responded. Words were not necessary. As a toddler, she relied on others to read the social and emotional cues of a situation and to guide her response. As an adult she continues to rely on others to do this for her.

Unable to Identify Emotions, Others Serve as the Emotional Anchor: She retains her toddler-like unconscious reliance on those in her vicinity; lacking her own internal emotional navigation system, she needs the emotional life of others to be the basis for her own. She relies on others to give her something to react to and against. As a result, she is intensely reactive to the emotional state and words of those close to her.

Passivity as a Way of Being: Unaware of her emotions and her personal needs, she passively waits to react to others, unless there is a performance at hand. If she has an audience, she will rise to any task—washing dishes, making copies, emptying the trash—she'll put on a show, delighting in the approval of her audience. Otherwise, daily chores hold little appeal. Routine tasks will slide by unattended while she focuses on that which will bring her status or stardom. She is passive about handling her own emotional needs because she is not consciously aware of what they are, and is accustomed to having her caretaker identify them and strategize around them. She is passive in providing for another person's needs unless these needs are clearly delineated for her. She prefers a strong and capable mate, one able to handle what she cannot. Or conversely she enjoys a submissive mate who will provide for her specific sorts of needs.

A Skilled People Pleaser: A two-year-old, dependent upon the attention of her caregiver to get her needs met, learns to read and please this all-important life-sustaining resource. Deep intuitive skills are honed early and perfected through years of practice. Her deft assessment of what is required to gratify her caregiver provides her with her greatest arsenal for developing appealing behaviors. Chameleon-like in her ability to shift even her accent to amuse her targeted audience, she is unaware of this deep intuitive ability. Conscious access to it is not readily available for daily interactions, but it is a great asset in the early stages of romance. A narcissist is so adept at this unconscious talent that she can target exactly what a potential mate needs to hear and give it. And so, many think they have found the "perfect" match—the hook goes in deep and secure. This intuitive ability will fade as the relationship develops into a reliable one for the narcissist, only to reactivate if the relationship is threatened and separation seems about to occur.

With new people she wants to impress, she's got an uncanny unconscious ability to discern how to get them to respond to her. In an ongoing relationship, people pleasing leads to situations where a narcissist makes agreements in the moment, but discards her responsibility later if it no longer suits her. She'll do this without knowing that she's doing it.

Furthermore, a narcissist will tell a complete falsehood because she believes that is what you want to hear or because she wants to to please you and avoid your perceived criticism.

Isabelle dated a man who told her he loved her, but later admitted that he didn't. He told her he'd said it because he thought it was what she wanted to hear. He probably said it to entice her to stay with him.

Or, for example, a narcissist might be late getting home and you call to inquire when to expect her. She might say she's almost there, that she'll be home in ten minutes. Yet from the ambient noise you can tell she's not even in her car yet. Rather than question her, you look at the clock and sure enough, she shows up later that her projected arrival time, but just about at the time she would have if she'd left work shortly after your conversation.

In this situation, it's tough to figure out why she would speak falsely about such an insignificant issue. What does she get out of the attempted deception, you may wonder. And then, too, it's an easy jump to assuming she thinks you are too stupid to figure out this little white lie. None of these is the case. In such an example, she's trying to please you because she's seeking approval since she knows you want her home sooner rather than later, and in this particular interaction you'll be pleased that she'll be home soon. That instant pleasure—even though it's obtained by falsehood—is what she seeks. Your likely reaction is outside of her realm.

Unable to Read Emotions, She Develops and Applies Rules: Lacking an internal navigation system able to read and respond to nuance, she compensates by observing and developing rules to live by. It's an "if this, then that" guidance system. She looks for patterns and repeats the patterns. This works as long as the social situations are not complicated. If more discretion is needed, a narcissist is at a loss and doesn't handle the situation well. Nuances are beyond her capability. She sees what other successful people do and does those things. Sometimes it works, but frequently, especially as the narcissist's world gets more complex, it doesn't.

She will also develop rules for who she is in the world. For instance, she may decide it's important to be seen as a "good boss" and then she'll decide what makes a good boss and attempt to put that into action. Or, a man might decide to be "the best business man" or "a great dad" and he'll consistently do whatever he thinks it takes to appear to be that. Given the different spheres in which we operate in life, a narcissist will have a whole set of self-definition rules. The elements of self-definition will stay relatively stable (and become predictable) through adulthood.

Needing to Rely on Rules, Simplicity Is Preferred: Lacking an internal navigation system that can assess nuanced emotional situations as they arise, being unable to respond flexibly and creatively in the moment, the narcissist seeks to figure out and conform to the rules of her surrounding society. She'll apply these rules in order to get by and get ahead in the world. In many instances, the notable skill of the narcissist for intuitively understanding what it takes to please people can make for huge professional success, and for initial relationship success. But as she ages, her world gets more complex. She may be workaholic because, once mastering the rules of the work world, she is more comfortable within its confines. It takes diligence to figure out the social codes and rules of other arenas; navigating just one is challenging but navigating multiple worlds would be exhausting.

Resentment: A narcissist relies on a significant relationship for assistance with social norms, yet will resent the person providing that guidance because the information or direction will be heard as criticism. Since the instruction comes from someone else, there is implicit criticism of the narcissist's lack of knowledge. This disparity of information indicates a gap between the narcissist and her significant other. The gap signifies a separation, an unwelcome threat. It's a double whammy; she feels shame for not knowing the social norms and she resents the gap she perceives when someone else fills in the blanks for her. This scenario is a losing proposition for all involved. She needs you but resents you for it.

There Is a Gap Between Words and Actions: A narcissist says what she thinks will get your approval but does what she wants to do. The gap between her word and her actions can be huge. On a daily basis, she says one thing and does another.

In the bigger picture, a narcissist does not necessarily live by the life philosophies she espouses; she does not create the life she professes to desire. Who she thinks she is and what she says about herself do not match how she behaves and the life she creates. For instance, she may claim to be the best listener there ever was, but in reality she's an impatient listener eager to redirect attention to a subject more captivating—herself. She may proclaim to love the outdoors, but finds reasons to stay inside and bemoan the confinement. It takes knowing a narcissist long term, and watching and listening carefully, to see that the distance between who she thinks she is, what she thinks she wants, and what she actually creates is great.

Undeveloped, She Simulates Authentic Emotions: Basic needs and basic emotions are deeply and authentically experienced. Observing the world around her, hearing other people's stories, she adopts the language of her culture, but in truth she remains unenlightened about her limited capability and experience. She will seem to the rest of us as if she experiences things in the ways of an emotionally healthy person. We are unlikely to know the difference unless we watch very, very carefully. Attempting to participate, reacting to others, she will discuss more complex emotional states in conversation despite not fully feeling them or experiencing them internally. She may put on a good show of complex emotion, but that show is based on observation, cataloging, and mimicking others.

Inability to Love: Stuck at being too merged with other beings throughout life, sophisticated states of experience cannot develop. In order to connect with another person, it is necessary to be able also to disconnect—this is what an emotionally healthy person does. The narcissist cannot disconnect as an adult if she did not form a separate sense of self early on. In order to *see* and truly appreciate another human it's necessary to be independent of that other person. Mature love is about connecting after having been separate. It is a vulnerable, heart-opened encounter that mingles two or more in a rich soup, blending the distinct flavors each person brings to the pot. Emotionally healthy people do not remain permanently merged. Merging is a temporary state that is deeply satisfying. The healthy union is highlighted by its transitory nature. After comingling we return to our separate self, anticipating the next reunion, perhaps, but not fixated by it. The contentment comes in the pro tem experience of connecting and merging. Being permanently merged, narcissists have a different experience, as do those with whom they are involved.

Attention Is Mandatory: In her world, lack of attention is interpreted by her unconscious mind as not existing, as being wrong, as being unloved and unlovable. Without constant attention, her very sense of being is threatened. Her inability to get and maintain the attention of her primary caregiver as a toddler actually was life threatening. But now, as an adult, her unconscious mind reacts as if that is still the case. This is too uncomfortable a place to live for long and she will do whatever it takes to resolve the discomfort. She will be unimpressed by those who are neutral toward her. If she meets neutrality or lack of attention in an existing relationship, she'll attempt to reassert herself by inviting any sort of attention she can get, positive or negative.

Positive Attention Is a Need: In her world, positive attention is a necessity. Her toddler self knew it was important to be praised—this meant she was approved of and therefore safe—and her adult self seeks the same sort of adoring approval. She is expert at arranging ways to get people to offer the attention she needs to feel okay in the world. She will associate with people she admires because they make her feel good about herself. She welcomes those who give her positive feedback and bypasses those who don't.

Initially, she idealizes those who help her maintain her self-image. Unfortunately, positive attention given to a narcissist is not satisfying for long. This attention must be constantly available to give her adequate reassurance.

Image Matters: A narcissist invests in making things look good and is skilled at doing what it takes to make the right impression. Her image is important. She is proficient at putting on a pretty face even when conditions are unpleasant. Since others are extensions of her, they are part of this, too. For example, a narcissistic parent will take a compliment of her child as a compliment to herself. Co-opting accolades ranges from having the right shoes and living in the right house, to pretending things are fine even when a huge fight rages behind closed doors. The person outsiders see might be very different from the one dealt with in a close relationship. Keep in mind: maintaining an image requires maintaining the appropriate markers of that world. If the narcissist is into grunge, then she'll work hard to maintain her grunge image.

All the Positive Attention, or Love, in the World Is Never Enough: A narcissist has an insatiable need to be loved and admired. No matter how much positive feedback, and love, care, and support you give to a narcissist, she will not internalize it, feel it, or remember it for long. A narcissist can dismiss years of compliments and gratitude as if they never existed. Remember that she does not source her own emotional self-respect, or self-care, nor does she have the ability to hold that appreciation or integrate it—that is in the hands of her designated caretaker. Her habit to have her needs met by another person is insatiable.

Healthy humans have self-respect, self-awareness, and a drive for self-fulfillment. Unable to source these on her own, a narcissist never gets enough affirmation, never gets enough attention from others. What someone else gives her is never enough, never delivered in the proper manner or at the ideal time, and never hits the mark. And because her need for self-actualization is outsourced, the memory of it slides quickly away. She gets her needs met by the people in her life, and if those needs are not met, she moves on. There is almost always someone else to provide for her, if even for a short time. She has no idea what she is missing, she just knows it's missing and she's looking for someone to provide it.

A Penchant for Self-Promotion and Performance: Since positive attention is a core need, a narcissist tends to relish and flourish in situations where she's the center of attention. Activities that are culturally sanctioned and have the potential to make her look good are attractive to her. From a private dinner to a podium or stage, she'll seem most alive when she has an appreciative audience. The larger the group, the less personal the encounter and the more comfortable she is. Public performance is an ideal venue for narcissists.

May Appear to Be an Extrovert: Our culture likes extroverts. Attempting to gain as much approval as possible, a narcissist is likely to appear to most of the world as an extrovert. Given that a narcissist also relies on isolating herself to cope with complexity and humiliation, it can seem as though you are dealing with two totally different people in different contexts—bright and extroverted with outsiders, withdrawn and subdued at home.

Negative Attention Provides Sustenance if Positive Attention Is Missing: Attention is attention, and a narcissist needs it in order to feel okay and alive. She'll prefer positive attention, we all do. It harkens back to her young days when all eyes were on her and the faces of the big people were all smiling. But with insufficient accolades or lack of positive regard, she'll provoke others into negative interactions. If negative attention was the primary sort available in her formative years, then she'll turn to it as an adult. As long as the spotlight shines brightly, it's less important whether her role is hero or villain. Negative feedback, despite its upsetting nature, is energy and is as useful to the narcissist's system as positive strokes. Conflict and negativity create intensity, an acceptable substitute for closeness.

Negative Attention Creates Unpredictable Responses: In her world, while any attention is better than none, negative attention is still interpreted as humiliating and shameful in a full being, physically intense way. This is highly uncomfortable for her, and drives her to seek relief as quickly as possible (even if she's the one who provoked it). When she encounters criticism or redress, she exercises a variety of coping tactics, all of which are designed to reassert her "rightness," or bring others into agreement with her way of seeing the world.

Criticism May Be Imagined: A narcissist will become frustrated by those who don't cooperate in giving her what she wants. She'll imagine slights when none are intended. When others assert their opinions or desires she interprets this lack of alignment with her viewpoint as criticism. She will either ignore or clash with those who act on their own behalf. Her significant other inevitably becomes one of these frustrating, dissatisfying people, as do many business partners, colleagues, family members, or employees. As relationships become long-term, she'll construe criticism where none is intended.

Intense Reactions to Perceived Criticism: Criticism is negative attention, and since she experiences it in such a visceral way, she'll frequently react strongly to what others might shrug off.

Disdain Will Become Apparent: Just as she hears criticism loudly, and can imagine it present when it is not, she offers her judgment freely. If something is not up to her standards, she feels no compunction about letting you (or everyone) know. She will expect your gratitude for her insightfulness, no matter how tastelessly she delivers it.

Uses Control to Get Her Needs Met: Living in the residue of a toddler's emotional reality, a narcissist's very survival is at stake in relationships. She craves positive attention, insists on her way, and requires people to behave in ways that conform to her view of the world. She will go to extremes to get people to behave accordingly. If others fail to do her biding she interprets the results as frightening and dangerous. Each failure ups the ante, intensifying the threat. She will escalate her tactics all the way to coercion and violence if necessary. She will be polite and diplomatic if that's the most effective method of getting her way. However, she will become prickly or nasty if necessary and escalate all the way to violence if it's important enough to her.

Consequences Don't Matter: A narcissist wants what she wants. She is not aware of the effect her actions have on other people because she is not aware they exist apart from her. Hence, she will not recognize consequences of her behavior on the relationship. She will not understand if you become self-protective. She may resort to extreme tactics to get her way without regard to the fall out.

Isolation Is Used to Regroup: When her rules for operating in the world are insufficient to keep up with the complexity or nuance of life, she'll temporarily isolate herself in order to repair. Isolation is her coping choice when life gets too overwhelming and when her rules aren't up to the task of providing adequate guidance.

Other Deep-Seated Problems May Be Present: A narcissist gets to a point in life when she realizes something about her life is not right. Along the way, in trying to cope with her issues, she may develop ineffective methods to cope. Addiction, crippling anxiety, and depression are prevalent among this population. Self-loathing and abusiveness are also common.

A Narcissist Develops a Rigid Mental Map of Others: Because you are an extension of her, and because you serve a caretaker role for her similar to the role of her early caretaker, a narcissist will not truly know another person. She will have an internal mental framework that more closely resembles the caring and correcting figure of her earliest primary caregiver than you. She will seek to push and prod you to conform to this template. That mental map may have the clothes and body that look like you, but her perception of you and her responses to you will have little to do with the true you. In a long-term relationship, it's likely that you will have fallen into patterns she's initiated for you that reinforce her assumptions about you. If you pay close attention to who you really are, independent of the narcissist in your life, you may discover a disjuncture of sizable proportions. You may uncover the person you truly are and realize you are not the person to whom the narcissist relates, nor the person to whom she wants to relate.

Therapy May Be Sought, But it's Likely Not to Be for the Narcissist: When a narcissist is part of a couple, and trouble develops, you may seek professional assistance. A narcissist will resist responsibility for her part in the problem. She may magnanimously agree to therapy anyway—because doing so will help to fix the other person. A narcissist engages in therapy, or anger management classes, or whatever self-help project is suggested for one of two reasons: If she gets help on her own (taking a workshop or reading a book or even going to therapy), it may be a way to placate her partner and prolong the relationship. Her other reason for counseling, particularly couples counseling, is to get help for her troubled partner (you).

Remember, the narcissist will not be aware of these unconscious motivations. If she goes to therapy on her own, she will have a delicate relationship with the therapist. Should the work get too close to her core issues or move too abruptly, a narcissist is likely to blow out of relationship and blame the therapist for something. Therapists who treat narcissists do so very gingerly and over long periods of time. Hopefully, a form of "re-parenting" will occur and the narcissist will develop the necessary neural-networks for independence.

A Marriage: Domination or Parallel Living, Not a Partnership: A narcissist seeks to control a relationship so that it meets her needs. If possible, she will dominate and control all aspects of the relationship and as much of the other person's life as possible. If attempts at domination fail, then two very separate but coexistent lives emerge. Authentic communication, intimacy and support will be missing. A partnership, based on mutual respect and give and take, simply can't develop.

Two Narcissists Together: If two narcissists are together, they can create a stable, content system because they both operate from the same set of unconscious premises. It can be a very strong, rooted situation for each party, if they are enough alike in tastes and preferences. They are comfortable being merged. They don't need separation, autonomy, and connection that individuated people need. They stay merged and so don't get threatened by their partner having a separate autonomous self. Therefore, they don't experience much of the disappointment and rockiness of relationships between a narcissist and non-narcissist.

Problems will arise, though, if one partner wants something significantly different from the other. The question becomes whether what the narcissist wants is more important to her than the relationship. As they grapple with the issue, closeness may intensify and satisfy their needs because conflict is a form of closeness. But the relationship can end if what one wants is different enough from what the other wants.

The Caretaker Narcissist: We tend to think of people in caregiving roles as probably not narcissistic; after all, care for others is being provided so awareness of others must be present. Yet, narcissists frequently choose to be in caregiving roles, and are able to create quite complex social rule books for themselves. All the basic dynamics of narcissism are present, with an added element of the narcissist as benevolent (and superior) caregiver, and the receiver as the needy one needing the narcissist's expertise. When this personality dynamic is present, the receiver will always be turned into someone who needs help, and the narcissist is the one to provide that help.

Most problems you experience with a narcissist hark back to the fact that in her unconscious conception of the world, she does not know that you exist as an individual. While in relationship with a narcissist, you'll be admired, then disdained or worse. Your relationship will feel disconnected yet intense. It will be confusing, frustrating, and full of conflict. You'll think there is something wrong with you. You'll strive to please and you'll fail. You'll be blamed for your failures. You'll be expected to accommodate without being considered in return. What you want will not become reality unless it's what the narcissist wants. Anxiety will be a consistent undertone of your life. You'll lose some of your own awareness of what you want and may be mystified by how hard it is to make things happen for yourself. Speaking up will be risky. You'll have little to no support at times when you might need it. You won't have someone to share your successes, and you're likely to have them ignored or diminished. You'll do all the emotional work for yourself and the relationship; you're on your own taking care of the narcissist in your life. You'll either succumb to being dominated and seeking approval or you'll deal with conflict. If the narcissist is your mate, you'll have an unsatisfying sexual life. Issues will arise over and over again and never consistently be handled in a new and more effective manner. You'll become isolated. But there is hope: understanding the frustrations and challenges of your relationship can help you have compassion for yourself and empower you to turn your attention to your future.

ENMESHED WITH THE NARCISSIST

THE NARCISSIST

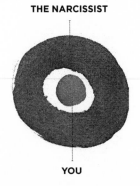

YOU

Emotionally healthy people, who operate with an awareness of others and take others into consideration as a matter of course, have a very hard time understanding that the narcissist doesn't realize that there is any one to consider other than herself. Other people are simply a part of the narcissist's personal equation, not separate from it. The narcissist's conscious mind may think she respects you, and may tell you she respects you (because that is the language other people use and the narcissist thinks she is the same); yet the narcissist has no concept of respect and consideration because her frame of reference is exclusive to herself.

"It's impossible to put into words, but it's like dealing with a person behind glass—you can see him and talk to him but you can't really touch him or be touched by him."

Chapter 5 | *Why Narcissism Makes You Feel Crazy*

Everything that's been described so far might explain why you feel so frustrated. Yet in order to understand a bit more about how being involved with a narcissist can be so crazy-making, it's helpful to look a little closer at some of the dynamics. This chapter will try to illuminate the confusion generated by being involved with a narcissist.

What Happens When an Individual Becomes Involved with a Narcissist (a Non-individuated Person)

If you are in relationship with a narcissist, you start out assuming he is within the realm of emotionally healthy. You have no idea that he is emotionally unhealthy, that he is merged with you in his unconscious processes. You'll assume that he is like most other people, where you are treated as a distinct person where give and take between two people is a matter of course. You'll have no idea how fundamentally different your narcissist is—he looks and seems pretty similar to other people. A person in relationship with a narcissist is not aware of being merged, and yet lives daily with its effects. Frequently, this dysfunction is explained away as what marriage or partnership requires for success.

Inter-relatedness cannot happen because there is no emotional separation. You'll assume you have affinity because all the appropriate markers are there, but the underlying feeling of closeness will be missing the majority of the time. A narcissist will hear about emotional relating from other people, will be able to speak the language of relationships, and have no idea that he is fundamentally different. You probably won't either.

A narcissist doesn't interact; he either acts or reacts. If you pay close attention to your own reactions when you are with him, you'll be able to discern a particular feeling. It's impossible to put into words, but it's like dealing with a person behind glass—you can see him and talk to him but you can't really touch him or be touched by him. If you're used to being around narcissists, it might feel familiar and no warning bells will sound for you.

A narcissist can strike the pose of any emotion, but the authentic experience will be missing. Instead, there are "simulated authentic emotions"—the motions without the actual emotions. This may be hard to detect, but it might be a persistent feeling of flatness or that something seems "off." Often a narcissist is busy reviewing his rule book, the "to do" list of actions appropriate to keep another person happy. "Just tell me what to do and I'll do it," is a common refrain of the narcissist. He is responding to you not in an engaged, interactive way, but rather in a "What am I supposed to do so you'll get off my back?" way.

For the receiver in a primary relationship with a narcissist, life feels flat and dispirited because there is no "other," no distinct individual with whom to return the relational volley with emotional authenticity. Instead, you become the stable backboard against which the ball bounces as he plays his best game. Step away from the backboard, start moving, and the problems begin. He'll meet you with his intellect and his rules to try to do what he thinks might placate you in a given situation. Sometimes it works, or convinces you of his earnest allegiance, but essentially, the relating falls flat. The appropriate actions might be present, but it still feels disappointing or somehow off the mark because it is not authentic. It's easy to miss what is actually happening, because it has the markers of socially appropriate, or familiar, behavior. He'll be frustrated if you are displeased with his rule-bound attempts to meet your desires. His frustration can often hook you again and force you to return to your position as the "stable backboard" and the relationship pattern that works for him.

When it comes to a "love" relationship, he may do what it takes to "show" love, but the actual feelings that motivate the motions are absent. He may say he loves you, he may think he loves you; he does not know that something fundamental is amiss and that love as most people know it is not possible with him. Often intimate relationships look picture perfect to outsiders; in that situation, the narcissist has been a careful observer and knows how to present as a caring mate.

If the relationship is a romantic one, the situation can be deeply distressing. The words and markers of love may be present and you are likely to think it means you are loved, yet you encounter contradictory behavior, you don't feel the love, and you don't feel "seen" or "gotten" or "understood." This may make you wonder, "What is wrong with me?" This confusion can be deepened by the fact that a narcissist may profess that you are SO special to him, and that you know you are special because he invited you to be the special one for him while he expresses disdain for so many others. What you've not known is that in agreeing to join this relationship you inadvertently joined his reality, excluding your own. You are now enmeshed, essentially one being on the unconscious level. In this position of mirroring you cannot feel love, because love is the emotional exchange between two separate beings.

A narcissist can never feel respected or loved enough; he's an empty vessel into which you pour your loving essence, but it runs right through with nowhere to land. He may present himself as wanting closeness, but he'll be clueless about how to foster it and will fail to do so. Again, you may think there is something wrong with you. You may try all sorts of tactics to get his essential attention, but you never experience the ahhhhh of contentment. Louise Kaplan, one of psychology's experts on narcissism, points out, "If lovers do not appreciate one another's separateness, love stagnates."

Consequences of Being Enmeshed yet Living in Two Very Different Realities

Having lived with yourself for a lifetime, you know yourself; you are self-evident. You know you exist and that while you may have many things in common with others, there is something distinctly "you" in play. The narcissist doesn't know that. In your reality, you exist as a separate person. In his reality, you exist as part of him (although he is not aware of this).

To those uneducated in narcissism, you assume he knows you exist since he sees you and talks with you and does things with you. It's difficult to wrap your mind around the fact that you don't exist as another person to him. Since to you, you do exist, you will assume you exist as a separate, unique human being to the narcissist; it's really only natural to do so. But, the fact is that his unconscious mind does not know you exist independently. You live in the same house or work in the same office, you interact all the time. You assume he knows you exist as a separate person. He may appear to be inconsiderate, or disrespectful, or thoughtless, or a poor communicator. It's natural to believe he's choosing to be this way and could change if he understood, or wanted to, or if you explained well enough, or begged enough, or got mad enough. Until you become educated in the ways of narcissism, you will not know that change is unlikely because of his need for someone else to take care of him at the essential level. He did not develop awareness to know that he can exist on his own.

The books and articles about narcissists say that a narcissist considers "you to be an extension there to meet his needs." A person not willing to supply these functional needs will simply be off the radar screen of a narcissist. If you are removed from the role of provider, by choice or by circumstance, the narcissist will take action to invite (provoke) you back to handle this supply for him. If you are still unavailable to meet the need, for whatever reason, you move off the radar screen and he will seek someone else to serve his purpose. Even if you move yourself off the radar screen, he may attempt to pull you back into his orbit as a source of "supply" if you are still somewhat in his vicinity due to shared children or business dealings.

A narcissist never leaves his own reality to visit in the world of another. If you are in relationship with a narcissist (and are not one yourself), then you are aware of another person's existence, differing points of view, needs, and distinct identity. Managing relationships successfully requires that you maintain self-awareness and develop awareness and memory of the others with whom you interact. You hold on to your identity and your reality, and at the same time can imagine, or at least attempt to step into, the shoes of the other to understand their point of view. You visit their reality in order to understand them. You ask what is going on from their perspective, and can inquire about their needs. This is empathy, and emotionally healthy, successfully individuated people do this naturally. In an emotionally healthy relationship, both parties move back and forth between their own and each other's reality, occasionally melding into intimacy with a shared reality. We are not all successful at this all the time, and we are not free of confusion as we make our attempts to understand and navigate these two spheres in service to finding common ground or agreement. The confusion and frustration that come with being in a relationship with a narcissist are constant; they are not the occasional experience, but the primary ones. But this may not be obvious to you. Trying to live in both his frame of reference and yours—bearing solo responsibility for bridging the two realms—becomes exhausting. It's like bending down to pick up the spoon over and over again for a two-year-old. It loses its playfulness with all that excessive repetition and no reciprocity.

A narcissist has no idea of his own unconscious framework and thinks he interacts with you as if you exist as a separate individual. If you asked him, he'd say, "Of course you exist, and I deal with you. What a crazy question—you're right there in front of me!" Yet, he doesn't have any way to anticipate the effect he will have on you. It may be hard for you to recognize this, because he may respond to what you say you want with ease and agreement and you won't be aware that he only does this if you initiate and if it works for him without much adjustment on his part. For example, when making plans together, an individuated person might say something like, "I can go to the 7:10 movie, what about you?" But the narcissist would say, "I want to go to the 7:10 movie." This can seem like a very subtle difference and if the narcissist is generally congenial it can go by easily unnoticed for ages, but over time it gets tedious.

This most basic fracture between your emotional reality and the narcissist's is likely to cause confusion, frustration, and distress for both of you—for very different reasons. The narcissist's need for you to maintain your balance and place in his system can lead him to escalating tactics and forms of intimidation. Violence is a last resort, but it is a possibility. For most of us, it is very difficult to identify the actual source of the problem. You may think you have "communication" problems; yet it is in fact a "reality" problem. Your realities are very different. In your reality, you exist and in his reality you exist as long as you are providing for him in some consciously or unconsciously needed way.

The fact that you hold no distinction as a separate individual will play out in myriad confounding ways. Being heard, considered, known—these are all basic human drives and it is infinitely bewildering to have these basic needs frustrated, especially by someone close to you. Tenacity, creativity, commitment, family dynamics, religious beliefs—all can play a part in your continuing effort to employ different tactics to make the relationship work. Unaware, you may stay invested in the relationship simply because you are attempting to achieve the satisfaction of being recognized as your own person, being seen as who you are, being validated as a human being. While these desires are normal, they are beyond the means of a narcissist to provide. Mostly it is difficult to conceive of such blindness and thus you are often stymied by your interactions and hooked into the fruitless search for recognition.

Emily explained her interactions with a narcissist like this: "It's as if I'm standing right there in front of him, but he can't see me. I'm jumping up and down, waving my arms, yelling for his attention, and he doesn't notice until he wants something from me. Then it's as if I come into focus long enough for him to say, 'I need a ride to work tomorrow,' and then I disappear again."

Frustration, confusion, anger, and conflict are likely in this sort of relationship. During an exchange with a narcissist, when he is showing his wares, you experience a subtle internal "jolt" triggered by something he says or does. Often your manners or basic good nature move you to accommodate, explain away, forgive, or simply overlook the slight offense. As the jolts continue and pile up, your response becomes less hospitable, less graceful and increasingly is filled with annoyance and anger. Finally, your attention gets riveted on the significance of these previously minor infractions. Anger becomes the common emotional undertone.

Sexual relationships can be disappointing because of the narcissist's inability to be curious about another's perspective (or even know there is another perspective). His gratification is his only interest. Mutual satisfaction may be an idea he's aware of, a theory he may even say he acts on, but truthfully it is not a motivating concept. His reality is, "If it's good for me, it must be good for you." Social training and the need to present an image might prompt him to seem solicitous; he may even ask you a question or two. If you do share your preferences with him, they are likely to be taken as criticism, quickly forgotten, or added to his rule book and applied without much flexibility. You may think you have intimacy, but mostly what you have is physical closeness. Be aware, though, that a narcissist may think it's important to become good at sex. In this case, the true motivation is performance, not intimacy and connection. The sex may be fun, but it can get lonely being on the receiving side of a performance.

Consequences of Trying to Negotiate

A narcissist is interested in having his way and getting his needs met the only way he knows how. He is not concerned about consequences other people bear. He will entice, cajole, maneuver, intimidate, coerce, and manipulate until he gets his way. If he encounters trouble getting his way, he'll engage in negative behaviors ranging from fussy to aggressive.

You may think that you have influence in making mutual decisions in your relationship, but the final word will be that of the narcissist no matter how it appears. Many narcissists will simply not invite your opinions or preferences. A savvy narcissist will invite your input. Watch closely and you may notice that you talk and express yourself, but it rarely makes a difference in the outcome unless he happens to agree with you. A particularly smooth narcissist can do this without your even being aware it is happening, especially if you are a person who likes to avoid conflict and isolation.

A sophisticated narcissist is likely to try to present his idea as if he's thought of it for you and as if it's in your best interest that the idea is being mentioned. If that's true, or if you're willing to see it that way, then conflict is averted. If you disagree and propose an alternative that he doesn't like, he'll bristle with negativity, and you'll feel that the stakes have been raised.

Frequently people give in at this point, simply to avoid the schism they sense under the surface about to erupt. It's probably a simple ingrained, unconscious calculation that having your way is not as important as avoiding the negativity that will ensue from insisting on your way. If at this point his tactics haven't yet worked, a narcissist will become obviously difficult. He will hold his ground and try to make you feel as if you are difficult, or wrong, or small, or inconsiderate, or thoughtless, or selfish, or stupid. Many people give up in the face of this. But, if you hold on to your point of view, dynamics escalate—starting with yelling, and moving on to mild or strong insults, or withdrawal, or walking out, or threatening, or physical intimidation, or violence.

The more you hold your ground, the more likely the narcissist will be to resist by withdrawing or by upping the violence. If you shift your mode of dealing with a narcissist from giving in easily to holding your ground more firmly, you'll experience push back from the narcissist and conflict will occur. We'll address ways to handle this in chapter 6.

Consequences of Being Your Own Person

A narcissist is different from successfully individuated human beings. Having bypassed the natural impulses to separate at age appropriate junctions in life, he has become a master of fusion. Should you resist or disagree with him you are wrong in his eyes.

You'll strive to be perfect, but you'll continually fail to gain his approval. A gnawing underlying feeling of being wrong becomes the familiar ground from which you operate. A sense of doubt clouds your confidence. A sense of anxiety fills your days. Your own once-trusted relational abilities, and even life skills, are called into question. The nature of the relationship erodes your sense of who you are. Your attempts to please him fall short so often that you lose belief in your own competence and abilities. Statements of disdain or criticism offered by the narcissist will be taken to heart. A narcissist will agree with you that you are the source of the trouble and collude with your self-doubt to undermine you. Unwittingly, you move from knowing something is "not right" to your being "wrong." This is an example of two people in close relationship feeling the same thing. However, for the narcissist, it's far better for you to "hold" this feeling of being wrong than for him to do so. Remember the splitting of good and bad parts? Here you get to hold the bad part so he can be good.

Consequences of Being Capable and Strong

Since you do not exist as a separate and distinct individual and he relies on you as if you are part of him, your emotions become his emotions and he reacts strongly to your emotions when they are focused elsewhere. His life process requires a dedicated "other" to ensure his course. It's as if you are the anchor to his ship. There he is floating at the top for all to see and admire, while you provide the grounding substance. Or it's as if you are the rudder, around which he moves and operates while you provide reliable stability for his navigation. Movement that might preclude his direct connection to you presents an intolerable threat to him. Therefore, if you focus on yourself, shift the attention from him, or move in some way other than his set course, he will react.

He wants you to be in an even-keeled state, paying attention to him. That leaves him free to operate safely, feeling secure and stable. If you have an upset or something to celebrate, or are the center of other people's attention, it interferes with your ability to function on his behalf.

▌ *He'll deal with it by:*

- trying to divert your attention,
- adopting your emotions as his own,
- offering up a quick, insincere apology, or
- attacking you while you're down.

To his unconscious mind, the retraction of your attention is basically life threatening; you are not there for him, navigating for him, and offering him safe harbor.

A narcissist needs you to be highly functioning because you are functioning for him. When you have an issue or upset, he does not have the awareness to know that the time you take to handle your life is but a brief intermission after which you will return. Feeling threatened by your emotional absence, he'll do what it takes to redirect your attention his way regardless of your need. As a result, you are often left unable to process your own emotions, you frequently end up dealing with his issues about whatever may be going on for you, and you lack support from a person upon whom you would normally think it is natural to rely.

If he can successfully take on the feeling state of the problem and get you to pay attention to him for that, then you have resumed normal operations where he is the center of attention and he can feel normal and secure again. Understanding and supporting you are simply not tools of his trade, although he may be socialized to pay lip service to your needs. For instance, you may have noticed that if you get mad at him, then he gets mad right back at you. Rather than dealing with what made you angry, you find yourself dealing with his anger, his issue (which may not have existed previously). Usually his issue gets big enough and takes enough attention that whatever got you mad in the first place is left unresolved. Or his anger will trigger your need to comfort him and maintain connection, so your issue will get left unattended. If you become very sad about something, you'll find that he becomes very sad too and you find yourself comforting him rather than being comforted by him.

Another reliable tactic often drawn upon by a narcissist is to offer quick apology without sincerity to get you off his back and return you to your optimal state for his service. A last and devastating device is to blame you for your own troubles while you are in the midst of trying to cope, thus adding to your difficulties.

Most of us assume that the people we allow close will

respect and support us. We assume that the people in our lives will be happy for our achievements and kind through our struggles. A narcissist will claim to support, respect, or love you, but will not be authentically pleased for your success because he needs to have your attention focused on him. There are a variety of strategies he might employ. In the moments of your success he will claim to like or love you, but then make fun of or diminish the importance of your successes, or fail to pay attention to them.

Or he may show disdain for you or insult you for something else altogether in your moment in the sun. He may have his own upset in order to pull the attention back to himself in the face of your individual recognition or achievement or attention directed your way. You expect support or celebration or acknowledgment and appreciation for who you truly are, but are met with blankness, blame, insults, or upset.

For the receiver, the dynamics of his need for you to be his center is significant. It means that your issues in the relationship with the narcissist do not get addressed or resolved. It means that you are not able to rely on the narcissist in your life for assistance or support in emotional matters. It means that you are not free to do your own emotional processing of things that come up in your life, unless you go off on your own. It means that you never have yourself to yourself to recharge or rejuvenate, unless you separate and isolate (as is his method). It means that your achievements are minimized. It means that you are not able to be the primary focus of your own celebrations. It means that a significant person in your life does not share joy in your successes. It means that you (and others) are diminished. It means that he will create upsets or conflicts to focus sufficient attention upon himself.

Consequences of Being Enmeshed

Lack of empathy, or the inability to understand and appreciate the feelings of another, is part of the basic narcissistic way of being. Since he is enmeshed he can't tune in to your emotions, he can't "read" you. What he needs or wants is the only thing he knows. Although you may articulate your desires and he may nod his head as if understanding, he cannot really respect other people's needs. So, he's likely to ignore or forget them, unless they mesh seamlessly with his own.

This creates all sorts of implications for day-to-day life. It means that a narcissist might violate your privacy without compunction. It means that he can't anticipate what might upset you. It means that if you are upset, he won't know how to calm or comfort you. It means making plans will be difficult; he won't volunteer information that might be useful, he will expect to be accommodated without offering to do so in return. It means that he will do what it takes to get his way regardless of the consequences.

If you can "read" the feelings of others, it's easier for you to attune to his feelings and near impossible for him to distinguish yours. Therefore, the feeling tone when you are together points more toward his position in the airwaves. This makes for an ever-present challenge to maintain your preferences, ideas, or opinions, whether or not you voice them, at least while he is in the vicinity. This balancing act requires a great deal of energy, depleting your reserves.

He'll invite you time and again to join in his feeling state in order to have the feeling experience for him, thus aiding him in recognizing his own emotional state. You can describe it. This may account for why arguments get diverted to him when you bring up a topic of contention.

What you want is not a priority to a narcissist. Not only is he likely to forget what he's been told, but when he does recall, he'll frequently remember incorrectly. His brain cannot easily retain what another person want if it differs from what he wants. In an ongoing relationship with a narcissist, expressing what you want can become a recipe to NOT get what you want. He simply does not let you have it your way if your way is different from his way. To do otherwise would be a tacit acknowledgment that you are separate from him, which is too threatening a proposition.

Life with a narcissist is generally disappointing and exhausting. Hopefully, a new deeper understanding of the dynamics at work can help relieve some of the pain you might be experiencing. Although it sounds bleak, there is hope for you, and the next chapter discusses how you can find relief.

"Your real power lies in changing your own perceptions, expectations, reactions, and behaviors. Relying on the other person to change is simply putting power in their hands and trusting yourself, your happiness, and possibly your safety, to someone else."

Chapter 6 | *Strategies for Dealing with a Narcissist*

Dealing with a narcissist can be a challenge. But it can be done and there are basic strategies that help. Most basic? Keeping your own emotional state in balance. If your relationship with a narcissist is a primary one, if it has a major impact on your day-to-day life, keeping yourself in balance will be critical. But staying in balance emotionally while dealing with a narcissist in a secondary relationship is also challenging. Either relationship—primary or secondary—can be addressed with the same strategies. In a secondary relationship you have more emotional space and more room to consider your options. Be aware that even in secondary relationships, the behavior of a narcissist can activate some pretty intense uncomfortable reactions in people on the receiving side. Distance does not necessarily mean your responses are not intense.

The major difference lies in the depth and tenacity of work you may have to do to create and maintain your emotional balance.

The Key Elements to Finding Relief

1. Remind yourself that she is not aware that you exist; this is not about you. It's amazing the relief that can come from that awareness. It's useful in that it allows new behaviors that are more effective to open up to you as a result.

2. Increase your awareness. Learn what triggers you. Understand your habits of mind that are not productive for you and the way you want to be and experience the world. Become aware of the narcissist's bids for attention and control and how they affect you. Your awareness of the dynamics will help you manage your life.

3. Reclaim your focus toward yourself. A narcissist invites your focus to be on her, and makes constant bids for your attention. Reclaiming your awareness for you and what you want will make for huge changes that provide great relief.

4. Set boundaries based on your needs. Determine what you want and how you will behave so you are satisfied. Decide on your goals for how you want to be as you go through life, what sort of experiences you want to have, where you want to put your attention both for yourself and for this relationship. Let go of triggers and invitations that seek to invite you to do otherwise. Minimize the amount of mental time spent on useless endeavors: anger that she's not acting the way she ought, wishing that things were different than they really are.

5. Reclaim your vibrancy. Reconnect to other people and activities that support you in feeling good in the world. Accept that you are experimenting with change, and that it is a process. You will not always meet your own goals for yourself. Acknowledge your successes, learn from your mistakes, tweak your approach, and keep moving forward to create a life that you love.

The rest of this chapter will provide an exploration of these key elements.

Avoid Using the Term "Narcissist"

It is useful—even crucial—that you keep your growing suspicions about your relationship with the narcissist to yourself. Do not tell the narcissist in your life that you think she might be a narcissist. Doing so is not productive. It is generally an aggressive, blaming move on your part. Your motive might be getting her to change through insight, education, or persuasion but your attempt will be counterproductive. This is troublesome territory and best avoided.

We tend to want to help, to correct that which we believe is wrong. But, a narcissist doesn't have the ability to self-correct because she doesn't have the ability to observe herself from another viewpoint. She can't assimilate feedback. Since narcissism is a socially unattractive behavior, she will not agree that she is one. She'll get offended and defensive, or turn it around and find a way to blame you, to make it your fault. Most importantly, she will be tipped off that you are questioning the relationship. She will take this as a threat; her response will negatively affect the dynamics of the relationship and undermine your ability to observe clearly and focus on yourself.

Prematurely sharing your suspicions about a potential narcissist could derail you. It's important to plan your next steps carefully and to base your actions on a solid and deep understanding of narcissism. Using labels is never helpful—and using labels with a narcissist can lead quickly to a severe deterioration in your relationship. Until you are grounded and sure of yourself, bringing up your suspicions or making accusations will be counterproductive. It will, predictably, sabotage your interests.

Sharing your concern about narcissism with other people is only productive if you share appropriately as a way to process and get support. It's easy for such talk to flip to gossip if you talk with the wrong person or for the wrong reasons. Railing about narcissism does not serve you to regain emotional equanimity. Gossip could get back to the person about whom you are concerned and undermine you.

Focus on What You Can Do

When you are involved in a relationship that is not working well, trying to change the other person generally will not work. Plus, any change a narcissist makes is likely to be seductive to you, but those changes will be short-lived. Your real power lies in changing your own perceptions, expectations, reactions, and behaviors. Relying on the other person to change is simply putting power in their hands, and trusting yourself, your happiness, and possibly your safety, to someone else. If you feel bad, even crazy, through your dealings with this person then turning to your own expectations and behaviors is the only place to find relief.

We believe that your best course is one that allows you to care for yourself—to nurture your own sense of well-being and effectiveness. This starts with examining and modifying your own expectations and behaviors in relating.

The foundation of all the information and tools in this chapter is a simple but powerful truth: Trust the narcissist to be who she is, and know that what's going on is fundamentally not about you.

Remembering that she is not aware you exist, although it sounds counterintuitive, can actually be the primary key to relief. This concept is simple and straightforward; it can, however, be a challenge to live out. The emotional triggers in your relationship can be deep and strong. Narcissists have a knack for flipping others into confusion and upheaval, causing you to mistrust yourself, to replay conversations, to doubt your feelings and sense of your interactions. It's as though you have an emotional loose tooth that keeps worrying you. Dealing with a narcissist from this upset place minimizes your effectiveness and makes you question your experience of your own life.

Start Carefully Observing

When you are concerned that a significant person in your life is a narcissist, start slowly. A quiet, centered period of observing is the absolute most productive thing you can do.

To begin, find a secure place to write your observations. Take notes. Assure your privacy, making sure your reflections are inaccessible to the potential narcissist in your life. You are in the first stages of opening your eyes and it can be a slow and foggy process. Writing down your perceptions helps track the different behaviors you detect, and helps you to recall what you've learned. Referring back to these notes will be useful throughout your process. Your new discoveries may be elusive—your mind is not accustomed to conceiving of this important person in these ways. Whether you use a computer, write in a journal, or take your notes on a flip chart or 3x5 cards doesn't matter—as long as you have one place to consolidate your observations. Eventually, lay it all out on a flipchart-sized piece of paper. This will help you sort out your impressions and organize your thoughts. Seeing it all in one visual sweep is clarifying.

Observe the Other Person and Yourself

Observe the other person's behavior. Do this for at least a couple of weeks. Refrain from comparing the narcissist's behavior to the information in the chapter describing narcissism. Simply observe and make notes without comparison. Monitor what she likes to talk about if left to her own devices. Study her behavior in dealing with you. Examine her underlying attitudes toward you and other people. Observe what matters to her, what is important to her, and her concept of herself. Simply observe what happens when the person in question is left to be and do exactly what is natural to her. This will provide you with a decent understanding of how she operates as well as her rules for interacting.

It can also be useful to take the time to understand her core values. A narcissist develops a relatively stable system, and it's possible to get familiar with that system through observation. Take time to assess her core beliefs about herself. For instance, some men want to be thought of as a "successful" or a "manly" or "responsible" or "creative" or . . . the list goes on. Women want to be perceived as any variety of things, from "beautiful," to a "good mother," "nice," or "smart" and other attributes. Pay attention to what she seems to want people to think of her.

Observe your own behavior. Pay attention to what happens inside of you, your thoughts and feelings, when your person of interest walks into the room or communicates with you. Notice how you feel and think while interacting with her. Compare this to how you feel and think when you are alone, with other friends, colleagues, or associates. Pay attention to the information you are responsible for providing to keep things running smoothly. Notice what she says that provokes you to either defend or attack. Identify the common patterns and phrases you use when responding to her. Observe the lines of thinking that you return to repeatedly in your own mind. Recognize when you take her bait and get into a disagreement. Determine when you shut down and what activated this response from you. Notice when, if ever, you are completely relaxed with her, being all of who you are. Write down your observations.

Take time to understand your particular triggers, those things that invite you into counterproductive interactions. Identifying the things that provoke and hook you, that have kept you stuck, can be very empowering. Mine this book for clues to understanding what impels you to interact in unproductive ways with the narcissist in your life. It might be useful to think of the various behaviors of the narcissist as invitations extended to you to act in certain ways. Consider what invitations are being issued, what sort of interaction is being requested. The purpose of understanding your triggers is to raise your awareness, and is the first key in your key ring toward having choice over how you spend your energy. Be assured that however dissonant and painful the interactions in your relationship, there are tools to help you handle it. Understanding your triggers is one of those tools, and a powerful one.

■ *Remember that these triggers can evoke somewhat predictable motivations in the receiver:*

- feeling unable to connect at an emotional level invites you to chase after the narcissist
- feeling the glow recede and wanting to be special again
- feeling disrespected and wanting to demand respect
- being discounted and wanting to be considered
- being ineffective and wanting to be influential, or to get it right
- feeling dismissed and wanting to be acknowledged
- knowing something has gone awry and denying reality or holding on to hope for change
- being confused and insisting on understanding
- feeling disdained and wanting to prove your worth
- feeling afraid and accommodating rather than facing fear

Once you recognize patterns of communication and behavior repeating, compare your observations to the earlier chapters in this book (or other books) that describe the basics of narcissism and the relationship between a narcissist and other people. Allow yourself time to process the conclusion you've drawn. Seek skilled professional input—it's likely to be helpful to you.

Accept the Reality, Update Your Expectations

Remind yourself to trust the narcissist to be herself, to act as she has before. Remember that she is fairly rigid, not flexible in her responses. Remembering this is useful. If the root of your unhappiness often lies in unrealistic expectations you have of the relationship, expectations that frequently leave you disappointed and frustrated, then accepting the reality of what you are dealing with, and changing your behavior is an important step in your self-care.

Narcissists tend to provoke people. Provocation produces knee-jerk reactions. The conflict that ensues requires your focused and intense attention, diverting you from other elements of your life. The narcissist successfully claims your attention, and you move into a negative, unpleasant state. Freeing yourself from this, or avoiding it altogether, is up to you. That's easier said than done, for sure. This process takes diligence. It will become easier with practice. However, the narcissist does not have to change for you to change your own behavior and your experience. You may not ever get over feeling incited every time the narcissist discounts or ignores you, but you may more quickly regain your composure and free your attention for other areas of your life.

▌ *Things to remember about the narcissist in your life:*

- Trust her to be who she is. Her mode of operation is consistent. Do not trust her with yourself, but trust her to be herself.

- Remember this is not personal; it feels personal but it really isn't about you. She'd be acting this way no matter who her partner, friend, or colleague was. You just have to decide if you want to react in the predictable way that leads to frustration. You may have to decide if you are willing to be the prime caretaker. Decide—are you willing?

- Remind yourself (frequently, if necessary) that for her, you do not exist. Who you are is irrelevant—what you do for her is what matters to her.

- Stop assuming she is like you. Do not expect that she'll have reactions and responses that make sense to you. Mutual interest and reciprocity are not part of her behavioral code, as you would probably assume. Concede that her reality is quite different from yours.

- Stop relying on her to do what you want or think she ought to know needs to be done. Stop attempting to take care of yourself by telling her what you think she ought to know or do. Realize that she is unlikely to act on or remember the things you tell her. She is likely to hear your input as confrontational.

- Remember that you and your narcissist live in two different realities and that from her subconscious perspective, there really is something wrong with you because she does not, and cannot, comprehend that you and she can have differing viewpoints. Try not to be surprised or take it personally when you are confronted with this.

- Be aware that there's not a thing you can do to alter her understanding of who you are. No matter how little you resemble her mental model of you, it's her mind map and she can only be in relationship with that facsimile and not with the real you.

- Notice that, unless you are in a superior role, you have little influence over her. You do not affect her. Realizing this can relieve you from having to try so hard and feeling ineffective.

Focus on Yourself

You can change the dynamics of your relationship by learning to focus on what you want—both in the big picture and for each interaction—and developing productive methods for achieving your aims. This is about knowing what you want and setting boundaries for yourself, your behavior, and your interactions. Clarifying your focus (and relating from the strength of that clarity) can have a profound effect on your relationship. It may take time to develop this habit of thought before action. Integrating your newfound awareness and operating differently is a process, quite doable, but not instant.

Your Big Picture Goals

It is extremely useful to take time to assess your personal goals for yourself and for the relationship and seek to act accordingly. Do you want more peace for yourself? Do you want more energy free for endeavors that interest or support you? Would you rather engage in conflict or maximize calm?

We base all of our recommendations on the idea that your world, and the world-at-large, are a better place if you are focused on maximizing your joy and human potential. Underlying an ability to do this is an emotional maturity that allows you to make choices rather than behave unconsciously using reactive unconscious behaviors that may or may not serve you any longer. People who are authentically themselves, and find joy and meaning in life, are simply happier people. We have found that equanimity, rather than drama and conflict, supports these efforts. Calm and peace allow you room to focus on yourself while interacting with reciprocity and compassion with those in your life.

When you discover you are in an important relationship with a narcissist, it is useful to take time to think about your own big picture. This may mean thinking not so much about your overall life goals and direction, but about who you are in the world and how you want to be and feel. You have choice over the emotions upon which you focus. If you aren't able to access that choice, then it can be useful to get help to sort things out. A therapist can help you increase your awareness and options.

Some emotions seemingly hijack us against our will despite our therapeutic endeavors, heightened awareness, and strongest intentions. You might seek help from a professional specifically versed in retraining neural pathways. Look for people trained in EMDR (Eye Movement Desensitization Reprocessing) or EFT (Emotional Freedom Technique) or Neurofeedback (Brain State Conditioning is one form of this).

Focus on Your Needs

People involved in a primary long-term relationship with a narcissist are adept at focusing on and adapting to the needs of others. People in secondary relationships with narcissists may not be as comfortable with accommodating, but may do so for practical reasons. Often it feels easier and more important to accommodate another person's wishes than to voice and negotiate your own desires. This repeated pattern of conciliatory behavior banishes personal wants to the background and eventually obscures them from your awareness altogether. Practiced over time, life becomes dull and barren.

If this is a long-term, primary relationship, your persistence in maintaining the relationship is probably reinforced by a variety of factors. You may believe you have no choice. You may highly value the relationship. You may have had what you thought was good reason to be hopeful. You may think it is important that others believe this particular relationship is flowing smoothly. You may be hooked into trying to get him to treat you well or give you his approval.

When something about this dynamic captures your attention, whether through extended or escalating conflict, lack of vibrancy, loneliness, or some other alarm-ringing awareness, it is time to pay attention to yourself. Focusing on your needs, distinguishing what you need from what the narcissist needs is key.

Start raising your awareness of what you want by taking time out from your usual routine responses.

▮ *Ask yourself these things:*

- What do I want right now?
- How would I do this if I were free to make this choice on my own?
- What's important to me in this situation?
- How is my body reacting right now? What's it telling me?

If your answers to these questions are elusive, take more time. Keep asking the questions and allow the space for answers to emerge. This may be unfamiliar ground for you, and it may take time for you to develop this awareness. It may be uncomfortable for you to pay attention to your own wants and needs in this way, but over time it will become easier. Women seem to be especially adept at going along to get along, and can have difficulty getting in touch with what they really want. Practice is useful.

Journaling is clarifying. Help from a therapist can provide objective support.

You may want to spend some time practicing this until you establish a reliable ability to tap into your own needs and wants. During this time refrain from taking any specific actions toward changing the way you handle your relationship, if possible.

Identifying your own needs and finding resources to meet those needs does not make you a narcissist. Narcissism is labeled "self-absorption," but it could more aptly be labeled "absence of self." A person who meshes with another person in order to know that he exists, certainly lacks a sense of self. "Healthy narcissism," or emotional health, refers to a person who has an awareness of their core, essential self, and is the guardian of their own interior experience. Such a person is a differentiated autonomous, free-standing individual. While recognizing his own needs and wants, he also takes responsibility for finding resources to get his personal needs met. As he goes about caring for his needs he is aware of other individuals around himself and responds to their unique personhood. His relationships, short- or long-term, are fluid, moving into connection and engagement then releasing and separating from one union to the next, all the while being aware of himself and mindful of others. This does not necessarily mean always complying with others' preferences; it simply means being aware of those preferences and those people.

Guidance for Interactions: Be Diplomatic

The most direct way to address your situation is to recognize what you need and then find a way to get it without relying on the narcissist to meet your needs. Of course, sometimes it is not possible to proceed without involving the narcissist. In this case, it's important to understand the narcissist's world and to think carefully about how to get what you want without triggering yourself or the narcissist into upset or conflict.

Relationships are built on a series of interactions. Handling interactions so that your experience is as satisfying as possible will change the nature of your overall relationship. Using these suggestions can give you a way to satisfy your personal needs and keep your relationship calm while maintaining your own integrity and taking the high road.

First, Think Strategically: When it's time for specific interactions, it's helpful to first get clear on exactly what you want. Identify your goals for this exchange. Getting to the point of clarity requires thought, reflection, and focus on what you truly desire for yourself. You may want to spend less time feeling angry. You may want to keep a child free from your conflicts. You may have a number of goals; some may conflict. Whittle your list to the most basic and fundamental; give these the highest priority. Once you know what really matters to you (aside from having the narcissist in your life be different), proceed with these goals in mind, and behave in ways that best help you to achieve them.

Before or during an interaction give your goals some thought—Some questions to consider are, "What do I want?" "Will this serve me?" "What do I want for myself and my family?" "Where will I be in five years if my relationship continues progressing in this manner?" "What are my children learning from this modeling?" Consider how you want to feel after the interaction is complete.

Second, Think Tactically About the Interaction: Think tactically about each interaction, and consider how to best meet your objectives in every situation. The approach described here may seem like giving up ownership of your personal desires, and that may bother you. But it's about giving up conflict, giving up your insistence that he be and behave in ways that are not possible for him. It's acknowledging what you've been dealing with all along while banging your head against the wall. This system brings your focus back to you and what you want, rather than diverting it to focus on placating or serving her. This approach affords an opportunity to have your needs met without upset. Experiment with the different elements of the technique and see which serves you best.

- Given what you know of what matters to her and what triggers her, assess her needs and consider her usual response.

- Decide what to say, what NOT to say, and how to interact in order to best meet your objectives.

- Reinforce any of the positive behaviors or attributes she has as frequently as you can. Just like most people (but for different reasons), she'll respond better to positive strokes than to negative. Never lie; say only what is true for you. If you are quite angry and desolate, at least summon up things to say like "You are something." She will take that as a compliment when you might have a different meaning. Take note, however; much of verbal communication is conveyed through inflection and intonation, so be most diligent in staying as emotionally affirmative or neutral as possible with whatever words you choose to use.

- Maintain a conversational pace that allows you to think while you discuss. You want to maintain an awareness of your own experience and your goals while you are engaged with the narcissist. You may need to slow the pace of conversation from what seems your usual natural pace, so that you can maintain awareness and thoughtfulness during the interaction.

• Avoid taking ownership of ideas by avoiding saying things like, "I think," or, "I want." Generate ideas as if they are neutral and came from the big idea bank in the sky. Use objective references instead of personal pronouns when making suggestions. Use terms like "It seems like . . ." or "Would it work if . . . ?," or "Maybe it'd be good to . . ." Create oblique avenues to introduce your ideas rather than owning them as your own. This approach is contrary to direct communication skills for a purpose. Tacit references diffuse ownership of the idea, and allow her to own the idea as her own, bypassing her need to contradict or control.

• Start by asking the narcissist for her opinion first. This allows you to see if you have common ground. If you can refrain from offering your opinion first, you will avoid activating the narcissist's need for control.

• If your preference is different from hers, focus first on any areas of common ground. Acknowledge her train of thought, or her underlying goal, or the premise of her idea. Acknowledgment does not necessarily mean agreement. Simply repeat her perspective out loud. Then offer a neutral observation about any issues with the idea, and ask for ideas on how to address those. "This looks complicated, how will this work?" "This will require participation, who will attend?" "Sounds like you have a busy schedule, when would you like to go?" Avoid claiming any of these ideas as your idea or your problem. Continue conversing with her in this manner until several alternatives emerge. Then suggest which way it might work to do it. But do your best to avoid personal ownership of the suggestion.

- Refrain from trying to convince her of the wisdom of your opinion or idea. Don't try to influence her or get her to understand and agree. Take "I think . . ." out of your vocabulary. Instead say, "It seems . . ." Say much less than you are accustomed to saying. Offer much less of your reasoning or your needs as rationale for convincing her of the wisdom of your position. A narcissist is adept at co-opting information for her own gains. If you offer your preferences or explain your reasoning, you are giving her information she can use to thwart you achieving your goals. Remember reciprocity is not her mode of operation. Bite your tongue.

- Develop key phrases that you can draw on during conversation. Have some specific things to say that allow you time to think. You may need time by yourself to consider how you want to respond; buying time can work wonders.

▌ *Some useful phrases include:*

"Oh, that's interesting."
"I don't know right now."
"I'd like time to think about that."
"I'll think about that and get back to you."
"How did you come to your decision?"
"What factors influenced your choice?"

These phrases provide a window of time and avoid contradiction while revealing the thinking of the narcissist. They are particularly useful in the workplace or during negotiations.

- Refrain from pointing out her failure to keep agreements, or any of the other problematic behaviors you've noticed. Observe, but keep your observations to yourself or share them with an appropriate support person. Sharing your point of view with her will simply incite her (or you). It won't change anything. Refraining will keep the waters calm and allow you some peace.

- Since a narcissist derives what she needs from both positive and negative strokes, choose which you provide. Not surprisingly, a narcissist's reactions to these different sorts of interaction are fairly predictable. Like most people, she is calm when she gets positive strokes, upset and contrary when she gets negative strokes. You are more able to cope with a narcissist when you utilize positive strokes than when you go for the negative ones. Using compliments and positive attention are more likely to result in more peaceful processes. Crucial to the success of this is that your compliment be sincere, not sarcastic. It may be hard for you to offer her positive feedback at this point. However, if your big-picture goal is to nurture more ease in your life, then this strategy is useful.

- Conflict requires energy and demands focused attention. Decide if that investment will provide the benefits you're seeking. Sometimes conflict is necessary, but with a narcissist conflict most likely will be a no-win proposition for you. You end up feeling bad, confused, blamed and thwarted.

- If conflict does arise, keep yourself safe. If you are in a marriage-type relationship, and conflict escalates, consider having conversations with third parties present, or in public places. In a contentious divorce situation, utilize the barrier of a lawyer to protect yourself. Be aware that the tactics the narcissist uses may escalate beyond what seems necessary or appropriate.

- If she's upset in your presence, provide no resistance. Listen to what she has to say and acknowledge it without offering alternative points of view. Let emotions calm down. Take some time to think before speaking or acting.

- Avoid being defensive if at all possible. Your instinct to defend or withdraw stirs up the narcissist's interest in closeness which she'll seek even through conflict. If you cannot shake your defensiveness, end the interaction as soon as you can, as amiably as possible. Don't pick conversation back up until you've thought through what provoked you and discharged any volatile emotions. Reassess your goals and come up with a new strategy or new resolve.

Third, Assess, and Tweak After Each Interaction: Review what happened, what provoked you and what upset her. Take notes. Progress may feel slow at first and your notes will help you acknowledge the gains you've made. Think about how you can adjust your approach in the next encounter, and acknowledge yourself for every small win. Making change in this phase is all about experimenting and practice, mistake, small success, practice, reminder, practice, mistake, practice, success, practice . . . Be patient with yourself.

Understand which habitual, unconscious reactions kick in during your dialogues. Assess how these behaviors impeded your management of the situation. Your old methods and modes of conduct will be re-stimulated at times—it's inevitable. The goal is to work with yourself to minimize your reactivity and expand your options.

Even a small change in approach should be considered a "win." Know that each step, no matter how small is a building block in the path of profound personal change.

A Note on Changing Your Habitual Responses

When you are in relationship with a narcissist, the unconscious mind is processing contradictory information and your own confusion and confused behavior may result. On the one hand, a person is inclined to create a primary relationship with a family member or business partner and that usually implies dealing with her in certain relationship building ways based on assumed reciprocity. On the other hand, the narcissist creates upset that kicks your fight or flight reaction into gear. Your unconscious mind is forced to deal with conflicting impulses of building the relationship and wanting to get away. You may find that you've been behaving in a contradictory fashion without knowing why. If the relationship has been intimate or long term or similar to something you grew up around, your habits of interacting are ingrained and will be hard, but not impossible, to sort out and change.

Be aware that narcissists feel threatened when the dynamics of their stable relationships change. This is true for all of us, but the narcissist is especially threatened because caretakers are so fundamentally needed. Big, abrupt changes on your part are likely to bring big, abrupt responses from the narcissist, whose goal is to keep receiving what you have always provided. When you change how you respond and handle things, she may start looking for ways to keep you in line and continue to get her needs met. Be aware that small changes on your part will be met with less reactivity, and big changes met with big reactions. Either can be manageable, as long as you are prepared. Be careful not to trip yourself with impatience once you begin to see the pieces falling into place. Clarity can be exciting, but moving too quickly may impede your developing awareness and skills. It may be preferable to get adept at interactions rather than speed up the pace; if you go fast, you're likely to experience two steps forward and one step back.

Essentially, these suggestions allow you to refocus your attention on yourself and build healthy boundaries. This will take time. For a while it will be hard to think clearly while interacting with the narcissist in your life. It will be reflexive to interact with your habitual patterns. The mind map of a narcissist is very hard for most of us to comprehend because it is foreign and counterintuitive to our way of relating. Be patient with yourself as you develop awareness. You'll need practice, time, attention, mistakes, and more practice. Think of it as if you are relearning how to walk—it requires conscious thought to make minute moves that you once took for granted.

Reclaim Your Vibrancy

You can do many things to regain a sense of joy being in the world. They sound simple, but it's amazing how elusive these sorts of activities are when you're engaged in a difficult relationship. As humans, negative episodes tend to capture our attention and worry our minds more readily than the positive. You may have to remind yourself to engage in rejuvenating activities. It is useful to structure pleasurable experiences into your life by committing to workshops or classes, or outings and blocking time for these things in your calendar.

∎ *Here are a few ideas:*

- **Rest. A lot.** Your brain is doing hard work as you reshape your relationship. Rest allows your neural networks to support this important creative endeavor.

- **Exercise regularly.** You may have been in a difficult relationship for a long time; if so, you may be physically and emotionally depleted. Depression is a common side effect of relating to a narcissist. Exercise of any duration and any sort helps the body and the brain to regenerate and provide you the energy necessary to move through this process and into your larger life. Yoga, biking, dance, swimming, running—all are good tools to get you back in your body, help you get reacquainted with yourself, and allow you to release negativity.

- **Look into issues of adrenal fatigue.** Your fight or flight system has been repeatedly activated and may be depleted. Integrative medical attention can help. Anxiety, over-reactivity, and inability to sleep all stem from the adrenal system being overtaxed.

- **Meditate.** By its very nature, meditation practice is centering. It brings your focus back to you, to your body, and away from thoughts that are likely to be obsessive and overwhelming. It helps to give you perspective: it reinforces the truth that emotions are real, but that emotions also change.

- **Eat well. Drink plenty of water. Take vitamins.** Highly nutritious, minimally processed foods will help you sustain your energy. In addition, quality nutritional supplements will ensure the necessary building blocks for optimal physical and mental functioning.

- **Notice how the people you turn to for support react.** A person's narcissism may not be apparent to them, they may not understand. If they are not supportive, refrain from sharing relationship information with them. If they are, let them be present with you.

- **Be aware that when a marriage is threatened, every family member will have their own point of view.** As your relationship with your narcissist changes, family members and close friends are influenced as well. Letting go of what was, both in reality and fantasy, requires conscious attention. All these people have their own relationship with the narcissist. Incorporating your changes into their lives will take time as well. Not everyone chooses to do the work that's required to be attentive. Some might not understand what you have been dealing with; others might. Once you share basic information, choose wisely about how much else you share. You may or may not find the support you hope for.

- **Create other things to think about.** When upsetting thoughts arise, or self-righteousness crops up, say to yourself "OK, thanks. But I'm going to think about something else now." Redirect your attention to uplifting pursuits. Such a shift might be small, but changing your mindset will change your life.

- **Pay attention to how your body responds when you are with the narcissist.** Where do you hold stress? Relax those parts when you are in a safe setting. Consider regular massage, chiropractic care, and/or acupuncture.

- **Get support.** Find resources to help you through this process. Maybe it will be a therapist skilled in narcissism, or a friend outside of your usual circle, a massage therapist, or nutritionist, or visits to a spa, making or viewing art, listening to music, dancing, gardening, or meditation, or workshops, or retreats, or all of these. Whatever you choose, find supports that bring you back to you; take care of yourself during a hard time. A supportive hand to hold through this process can be invaluable.

- **Do whatever is legal and healthy that brings you joy.** If you aren't sure what that is, experiment. Get out in nature. Get your body moving. Tap into your creativity. Rekindle your social life. Garden, paint, collage, get in touch with old friends, take up piano, clean out your closet, reorganize your office, woodwork, fish, write. Simply find things that you find fun, and do them.

You can fundamentally improve your quality of life by making changes that can help you reclaim your own place in your life and relationship. These changes may provide you enough relief that you want to maintain the relationship, or finding some relief might give you the strength to end this particular phase of the relationship. The next chapter will provide ideas that will help you consider your future. These ideas can increase your ability to make choices about your own behavior, lessen the pain you feel, and give you more personal freedom, no matter which way you decide to go in your relationship.

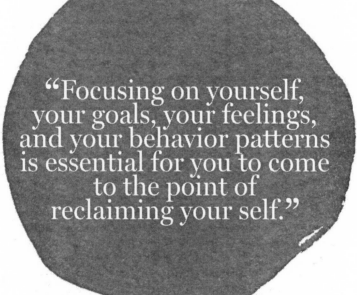

"Focusing on yourself, your goals, your feelings, and your behavior patterns is essential for you to come to the point of reclaiming your self."

Chapter 7 | *Your Future*

Anyone who has been involved with a narcissist has to think hard about how to handle the relationship going forward. Some of us have narcissists in our family or workplace and must learn to coexist. Others may have room to make a choice to distance from a narcissist. Everyone's options are different based on their particular circumstances. There is no "one size fits all" approach. Everyone's perception of their own situation and what is best for them and their family is different, and these things change with time and circumstance. Many of us want to avoid inadvertently developing primary relationships with narcissists in the future. This chapter is designed to address a variety of issues you face as you consider what the future holds.

If You Stay in the Relationship

Sometimes, quitting your relationship with a narcissist is not an option. Your father is your father, your sister is your sister, your business partner is your business partner. For others, severing the relationship may not seem an option for a variety of reasons: you have a family and want to maintain it, your financial situation is complicated, facing the conflict of severing ties may be too much. If you do not end the relationship, you can still take good care of yourself. You can choose how you handle yourself. You may be able to choose how often you interact, and you can influence the nature of the interactions by setting clear boundaries for yourself. You can acknowledge the things the narcissist is good at, and focus on tapping into those while you avoid running headlong into his weaknesses. Narcissists can be fun and handy to know, if you know what you're doing.

Although this book has focused on difficult relationship dynamics, the fact is that there are many highly functioning narcissists in the world. Narcissists can be excellent at their chosen professions (even if that profession is therapy), and not all of them have conflicted or troubled relationships. Some narcissists develop very sophisticated rule books that serve them well even in complex situations, and conflict can be minimal. These narcissists may have rather successful long-term relationships. That sense of essential connection may be lacking and you may wonder what's "off" but the narcissist may well be someone you want to keep in your life, or maintain in your employ.

Maintaining the relationship takes consistent focus on knowing what you want. It means relating in ways that keep the system between you calm. It hinges on maintaining clear boundaries. Monitor yourself for times when you feel you are conceding ground and might be uncomfortable in the aftermath. Simply change course. If some plan does not work for you, even if you've already agreed to it, simply say "You know what, that's not such a great plan after all. How about if we handle it differently," and allow the conversation to unfold. Remember the guidelines offered in the earlier chapters. Be aware of times that you are doing favors for the narcissist. If these favors are inconvenient for you and you'd rather not do them—don't. There's no need to make a big deal about it, simply bow out without fanfare or drawing attention to the matter.

Minimizing drama between you will go a long way toward giving you a peaceful quality of life. It can be hard to let go of the "I" in your sentences but doing so may surprise you with its effectiveness. Minimizing drama does not mean giving up what you want or going along to get along, it simply means using conversational techniques that take invitations for conflict out of the equation. It also means developing your personal resources so that you are not thwarted by trying to rely on the narcissist in your life to fulfill your needs.

To minimize drama in your external relationship, you may need to give your internal drama queen plenty of room to rage. If you need to have a temper tantrum for yourself about how enraged you are, or how hard it is, or how unfair, or how wrong it all is, then do so. Stomp your feet while you are by yourself (or with a trusted friend or therapist) and then pick yourself up and figure out how to behave appropriately in the situation you face. Fully acknowledging your own feelings can do wonders: It can free you to think more clearly about how to handle things. Pushing your feelings away and trying to be appropriate before you even know how mad you are will simply invite your inner drama queen to find ways to get out and be seen. Her thoughts will come out of your mouth at inopportune moments and may undermine you.

Allow yourself ample time for recovery after each interaction with the narcissist in your life. Even if you use all the suggestions in this book, it will still be aggravating to visit the reality of the narcissist. Even after years of intellectual understanding of the ways of the overly self-absorbed, you can still get triggered or annoyed at the tedious task of self-management. If a narcissist parent comes to visit, after they leave spend time journaling, talking with an insightful, compassionate friend, unwinding, or cutting yourself slack when you are off your game for a few days.

If you are an adult with options about how often you interact with the person in question, you may think about spacing visits out. Physical distance from a narcissist can make it a lot easier to manage the relationship. Energy and effort are required to deal with a narcissist in a primary relationship and taking care of yourself may mean interacting infrequently, or possibly only at times when you are adequately resourceful.

Will Therapy Help?

A narcissist usually engages in therapy, or anger management classes, or some other self-help assistance for one of two reasons: they either want to placate you and prolong the relationship, or they want to fix you. The narcissist is as unaware of these motivations as he is of being desperately dependent on your resourcefulness. But unless the narcissist invests years of effective therapeutic work on himself, even though some of the surface elements may show signs of improvement for a limited time, the core issues and patterns remain. It is common for a narcissist to end the therapeutic relationship if/when the truly core issues are at hand.

Narcissism can be a challenging issue for a therapist to recognize and treat. Narcissists are skilled at creating good impressions and their charm can be effective on therapists as well as on lay people. The very structure of therapy, where the client does most of the talking and is the focus of attention, may mask narcissism to the therapist: self-focus is expected. While psychotherapists receive professional academic training, narcissism can be most apparent to those who've grown up with it or been on the receiving end of it in a significant relationship, and gone on to learn and heal from it—such people are true students of the clinical disorder and recognize the attendant visceral cues it stimulates in them.

A narcissist can easily mask his troubling aspects from outside observers; these become most obvious when you are on the receiving end of a narcissist's behaviors and you experience the jolts and frustrations associated with being in that relationship.

If you are in couple's counseling, both parties have issues that need work: a non-narcissist becomes enmeshed with a narcissist because of their own history. If you are on a journey of healing, it's likely that the issues that brought you to the relationship with a narcissist can be understood and addressed. Learning what part of you was attracted to this person and understanding how you have adapted are worthwhile lessons. Having your best teacher (the narcissist) at hand during the therapy process allows opportunity for close observation with a familiar source. When you have absorbed all you possibly can and deepened your understanding of yourself and the narcissist in your life, you may then want to decide how to proceed with your relationship.

If You Want to End the Relationship

Once you consider everything, you may decide that it makes sense to end or distance yourself from the relationship. You may be able to end a relationship with a narcissist in situations where no future contact is necessary, and the narcissist gets the needs you supplied met elsewhere. You may only be able to create some relieving distance in situations where ongoing dealings are necessary. In either case, handle yourself with the utmost diplomacy and care. Ending a significant relationship with a narcissist, particularly of a romantic nature or business partnership, is best handled with serious attention. When a narcissist knows an important relationship is threatened his familiar patterns of behavior may turn negative and aggressive behaviors escalate. You must be aware and prepared.

Again, remember to avoid the use of psychological labels in discussion. Official diagnosis is best left to professionals for treatment purposes. To use such categories in conversation with a narcissist is counterproductive. No one likes to be pigeonholed or called names. And, "narcissist" is an unflattering description. Sometimes, when a narcissist is confronted with their problematic behavior, he might acknowledge the possibility and may even take steps to address issues—this can be more complicated for you because it may spark hope that change is on the way.

Most people are well served by laying the groundwork for their exit prior to bringing it up with the narcissist. This allows you the time to work out whatever knotty problems confront you as you disentangle your lives. A threatened narcissist is aggressive and intimidating. This can likely cloud your thinking and complicate your ability to react. The groundwork you laid in developing neutrality toward your narcissist is essential at this pivotal juncture. The narcissist easily recognizes abrupt shifts of attitude or behavior as a threat to his resources. Therefore, taking time to notice his behaviors, your responses, your self-talk around the interactions, and your trigger points while developing strategic interventions will serve you well as you plan and follow through with an exit strategy.

Do not be surprised if you experience conflicting feelings as you seek to end the relationship, particularly if it is a primary one. It seems to be a human trait to fight hard to keep whatever you have even when whatever you have is not enough. This is true in any circumstance where there are scarce resources; it's also true for a relationship that does not provide you with enough. We seem to be hardwired to hold on tight in the face of lack. When it's a primary intimate relationship we stay and make it work because to our animal brain being without a mate is life threatening. Letting go is hard work.

If you are ending an intimate relationship, it is likely your narcissist will hook up with another partner quickly. This can be confusing, insulting, and invalidating—open invitations for self-doubt and self-criticism. Look at it this way, though; since his needs are being met elsewhere it allows you more time and space to reclaim yourself. Though the process of self-reclamation may be challenging, it is critically important to your well-being. This personal recovery is especially necessary as prevention to filling the void left by your narcissist with another equally charming, brilliant, insatiable star.

It is possible that ending your commitment to the relationship may not end the narcissist's involvement with you. A narcissist may establish other primary relationships, but if your personality was strong enough or the supply provided by the new relationship is not enough, the narcissist may return to you as a source. This may take on the form of escalating conflict if you must grapple with common issues but do not agree with each other (which is more likely to happen after you've ended the relationship).

If you are married and decide to end the marriage, it would be wise to get a solid understanding of the divorce process, retain a lawyer, have a handle on your finances and be able to access all your financial documents in preparation. Think through your preferences regarding the decisions that will have to be made. Do as much as possible of this pre-work quietly on your own in order to give yourself time to come to terms with the issues confronting you. Divorce is fear inducing, and facing those fears on your own without the additional pressure of an aggressive narcissist is self-protective. Once you raise the prospect, consider keeping the fact of your prep work private.

If you live in a state that allows for the collaborative divorce process, consider that route carefully. It is an excellent option in many situations but is a process that relies on face-to-face negotiation, which is a difficult proposition with some narcissists. It can present a particularly difficult challenge because of their sense of entitlement, disregard for consequences, inability to see another's situation, and tendency to demean. Furthermore, your old habit of giving in may want to reassert itself. If you were successful at negotiation and conciliation, you probably would not be seeking divorce. The narcissist's limitations in seeing or accepting another's point of view is a major handicap in the collaborative divorce process. This might not be so if the narcissist deeply values being seen as a "good guy" in which case the process might work out well for you.

If mediation is to be part of the process, insist on being in separate rooms. This physical distance will allow you to keep your thinking aligned with your own best interests and helps you avoid regressing into old familiar patterns under the stress of such intense dialogue. Mediation sessions are frequently marathon affairs that can easily re-create old patterns and cloudy thinking. Protecting yourself by creating a physical buffer will help stabilize your equilibrium.

If you share children, and successfully divorce, you may expect ongoing conflict to occur. Despite the physical distance you've created, despite the fact that another primary partner may be in the picture, you are likely to still loom large as a source for the narcissist. The narcissist may once again see you as the source of his problems, or as the solution to his problems. You are still a primary relationship for each other, despite your distance. Your daily interactions will be limited and if a disagreement arises, you may feel clearer about your position. Just know that disagreement still triggers all the familiar patterns, and emotions can once again escalate beyond what might seem appropriate to the situation. If this happens, draw upon all your ideas and resources to get you through the rough patch. Remember this is not really about you, no matter how personal it might seem. Maintain your politeness and your boundaries no matter how blustery and intimidating the tactics used against you become. Get appropriate resources to help you.

Healing

Allow yourself time to recover after intense involvement with a narcissist. You can benefit from time to process your experiences; the more primary your relationship, the more time you will need.

Give yourself space to reflect. You may end up in a long-term relationship with a narcissist because elements of the narcissist's relational dynamics are familiar to you. Your own pre-conscious developmental template determines how well you match up to the needs of a narcissist. If you are highly attentive and accommodating to the needs of others or if you are overly responsible, your traits appeal to those who need a constant competent caregiver. If you are uneasy with intimacy or uncomfortable with attention directed toward you, accommodating the emotional distance of a narcissist may seem like second nature to you. If you are easily distracted by or sensitive to the opinions of others, capturing your attention and good opinion will provide the perfect challenge for a narcissist. These all set an inviting stage for the significant charms and entertainment of a narcissist.

If you grew up to develop one or several of these traits, you probably had trouble accepting attention. Though you, like all of us, want attention, for you this attention probably came with trouble attached, and now it is laced with apprehension for you. The early mixed message of "come close, go away" that you received meshes beautifully with the conflicted needs of a narcissist. If you grew up without adequate emotional mentoring, you will have compromised abilities for recognizing and resolving your own emotions. In such cases you carry an ever-present anxiety that can overshadow other emotional states. You are alert and watchful, and your vigilance serves you when you are on dangerous terrain. Caretaking and appeasement are your responses, and you are motivated to avert trouble by pacifying others. You exert an immense personal effort in your attempts to please. This form of self-protection is your way to keep negative attention, criticism, control, and capriciousness at bay.

In adulthood, hypervigilant caretakers usually develop into highly independent, self-reliant people. On the surface, these individuals seem very capable and easygoing. They are especially able to get along with difficult personalities. Self-reliance is a useful and admirable quality but when it is employed as a protective shield to exclude others, it can be a real liability. It leads you to perceive others as untrustworthy or downright dangerous. For you, because it has been so often paired with negative consequences in the past, support is suspect, and hard to accept. Because the narcissist gives so little support in a relationship, these two dynamics are a perfect match.

If you are a capable person, willing to provide accommodation, and a strong emotional anchor, one who is willing to provide what another person needs, you are exactly what a narcissist needs in order to survive. Balancing another person's all consuming self-interest with your own counterweight of total self-reliance works well in a narcissistic relationship. This lasts as long as you maintain your stamina for pleasing others and doing without for yourself—but this is a difficult combination to sustain.

Although the narcissist seems permanently consigned to his impaired relational framework, you may not be permanently consigned to your situation. You can change and heal. Commitment to learning about yourself, a willingness to experiment with your own internal state and your reactions to others provides you with the curriculum for change. You can relearn how to regulate your personal state in the presence of other people. You can stay attuned to the emotions signaled to you by your body, you can persist with attending to your own uncomfortable emotions, you can quiet your mind. All these are tools that move you on your way to healing. Over time, and with practice, your anxiety with others will dissipate, your ability to read your own emotional state in the moment will increase, your ease with holding your boundaries and taking care of yourself will improve, and your ability to navigate on your own behalf will be honed.

How to Avoid Narcissists in the Future

Once you've realized that you've been in a narcissistic relationship, you're likely to wonder "How can I stay out of this sort of relationship in the future?"

There are two ways to do it. One way is to develop a solid understanding of the narcissist's danger signs—and maintain a cushion of distance from people who exhibit those troubling qualities. The other way is to heal yourself so that you'll no longer be attracted to, or as attractive to, a narcissist.

Keep in mind that you won't avoid all narcissists, nor would you want to. Attempting to do so would narrow your world, and require a constant discrimination that is unrealistic and unappealing as a way of being. They can be fun, smart, entertaining, socially networked, and accomplished. Yet, you will want to use discretion in how many of these relationships you want to tend and how deeply you'd like to be involved because of the nature of emotional bonds required.

While you are in the process of recovery, rely on a basic checklist when you consider new relationships, whether they are work-related, friendships, or romantic. You may find it hard to discriminate in the very beginning of relationships. Spend time getting to know someone in a variety of circumstances and settings, both fun and challenging. It's worthwhile to make this kind of investment before you decide to commit to a long-term arrangement. Use the quiz in the front of the book as a reference to help you consider a new person in your life. If you find you don't really know if someone exhibits the warning signs, take that as indication to continue getting to know them without commitment until you're confident of their personality.

Some narcissists are so obvious as to be spotted easily not only by those who are educated in their ways, but even by those who are uninformed. Other narcissists (which we've referred to as *subtle narcissists* and are called *covert narcissists* by others) are harder to recognize; identifying them requires knowledge, time, and experience. If in the past you have been a good fit for a narcissist, and you meet someone new who feels like a perfect fit, be aware—this can be an indication of old unconscious patterns clicking into place.

Likewise, if in the past you were a fit for a narcissist, be on the lookout for a relationship that feels unfamiliar, possibly uncomfortable—these could be signs of support and reciprocity that are new and unfamiliar to you. If you meet someone new, offer yourself the gift of time. Allow your relationship to develop beyond the shiny and new. Be curious about your own experience with others. Invest your time in getting to know someone well. Pay attention to how your openheartedness is received and reciprocated. Commit your heart after time and experience informs you if your relationship has the chance to be healthy and mutual.

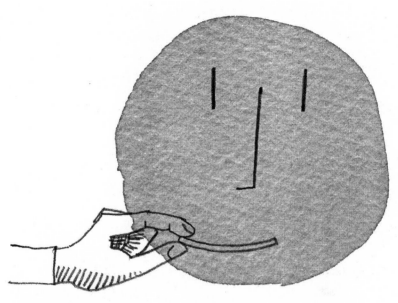

Final Thoughts

It may seem paradoxical that relief from dealing with an overly self-absorbed person comes from energy spent focusing on your own self. However, attending to your own goals, acknowledging your own reactions and emotional fallout, and caring for your daily needs does something very important: it puts you back on the map as being a worthwhile person who has unique gifts and who can be in an intimate relationship with another without becoming off-balanced and enmeshed. Focusing on yourself, your goals, your feelings, your behavior patterns is essential for you to come to the point of reclaiming your self. We hope the information and ideas presented in this book help to alleviate your pain, and set you on a path to greater personal freedom.

Recommended Reading

Borderline Personality Disorder:

Stop Walking on Eggshells: Taking Your Life Back When Someone You Care About Has Borderline Personality Disorder
Paul T. Mason, MS and Randi Kreger
New Harbinger Publications, Oakland, CA, 1998.

Sociopathy (aka. psychopathy, anti-social personality disorder):

The Sociopath Next Door
Martha Stout, Ph.D.
Three Rivers Press, 2006.

For another take on narcissism:

Why Is It Always About You? The Seven Deadly Sins of Narcissism
Sandy Hotchkiss, LCSW
Free Press, Division of Simon & Schuster, Inc., New York, 2002, 2003.

Emotional Life:

Loving What Is
Byron Katie with Steven Mitchell
2002, Three Rivers Press, New York, 2002.

The Gifts of Imperfection: Let Go of Who You Think You're Supposed To Be and Embrace Who You Are
Brene Brown, Ph.D., LMSW, Hazeldon
Center City, MN 2010.

Happiness: Essential Mindfulness Practice
Thich Nhat Hanh
Parallax Press, 2009.

Decreasing Conflict:

What Shamu Taught Me About Life, Love, and Marriage
Amy Sutherland
Random House, New York, 2008.

Bibliography

Bowlby, John. *A Secure Base: Parent-Child Attachment and Healthy Human Development*. New York: Basic Books, 1988.

Bowlby, John. *Attachment*. Second. New York: Basic Books, 1983.

Bowlby, John. *Separation: Anxiety and Anger*. New York: Basic Books, 1976.

Cline, Foster, and Jim Fay. *Parenting With Love and Logic*. Colorado Springs: Pinon Press, 1990. 271.

Cline, Foster W., and Jim Fay. *Parenting Teens with Love and Logic*. Colorado: Love and Logic Press, Inc., 2006.

Cozolino, Louis. *The Neuro-Science of Human Relationships: Attachment and the Developing Social Brain*. New York: W.W. Norton & Co., 2006.

Diagnostic and Statistical Manual of Mental Disorders: DSM-IV. Fourth ed. Washington D.C.: American Psychiatric Association, 1994.

Erikson, Erik H., and Joan M. Erikson. *The Life Cycle Completed*. Extended Version. New York: W.W. Norton & Company, Inc., 1998.

Faye, Jim and Dawn Billings. *From Innocence to Entitlement: A Love and Logic Cure for the Tragedy of Entitlement*. Colorado: Love and Logic Press, Inc., 2005.

Karen, Robert. *Becoming Attached: First Relationships and How They Shape Our Capacity to Love*. New York: Oxford Press, 1998.

Levin, Pamela. *Cycles of Power: A User's Guide to the Seven Seasons of Life*. Ukiah: The Nourishing Company, 1988.

Salter Ainsworth, Mary D., Mary C. Blehar, Everett Waters, and Sally Wall. *Patterns of Attachment: A Psychological Study of the Strange Situation.* New Jersey: Lawrence Erlbaum Associates, 1979.

Seigel, Daniel. *The Developing Mind: How Relationships and the Bain Interact to Shape Who We Are.* New York: Guilford Press,

Siegel, Daniel, and Mary Hartzell. *Parenting From the Inside Out.* New York: Penguin Group, 2004.

Siegel, Daniel J. *Mindsight: The New Science of Personal Transformation.* New York: Bantam Books, 2010.

Stern, Daniel N. *The Interpersonal World of the Infant.* Basic Books, 2000.

About the Authors

Tina Moody is a graduate of Duke Divinity School and The Fielding Graduate Institute. She has been a practicing psychotherapist for 30 years with experience in the faith, prison, and hospital communities. Her real-life experience with narcissists of many stripes deeply informs the insights of this book. She promotes personal growth, authenticity, and respectful living. Find Tina's practice at www.lifepractice.net.

Melissa Schenker is a work/life coach and holds an MBA from the Sloan School of Management at M.I.T. She has 15 years of experience helping clients navigate the intersection of their work and personal worlds. Work life satisfaction, full engagement in life, and authenticity are her motivations. Her practical point of view infuses this book with a refreshing clarity. Find Melissa's practice at www.worklifenow.com.